Martha Stewart's

PIES & TARTS

Martha Stewart's

PIES & TARTS

PHOTOGRAPHS BY

Beth Galton

DESIGNED BY

Henrietta Condak

CLARKSON POTTER/PUBLISHERS
NEW YORK

To my daughter, Alexis Stewart,
who loves to make pies and tarts
but never eats them

Published by Clarkson Potter/Publishers, New York, New York.
Member of the Crown Publishing Group, a division of Random House, Inc.

www.crownpublishers.com

Printed in Japan

Library of Congress Cataloging-in-Publication Data
Stewart, Martha.
Martha Stewart's pies & tarts.
Includes index.
1. Pastry. I. Title. II. Title: Martha Stewart's pies and tarts.
III. Title: Pies & tarts. IV. Title: Pies and tarts.
TRX773.S85 1995 641.8'652 85-12048

ISBN 0-517-58953-2

10

Acknowledgments

A BOOK SUCH AS *PIES & TARTS* REQUIRES A TREMENdous amount of work and the concentrated efforts of many people. I would like to express my thanks to everyone who helped with this wonderful project. My heart-felt thanks to Beth Galton for her extraordinary photographs; to her assistant Marcus Tullis for his strength and careful attention; to Kathy Powell, my editorial director in Westport, for her organizational skills and baking prowess; to Jane Stacey, Marsha Harris, Wendye Pardue, Jennifer Levin, Donna Scott, and Marinda Freeman for their baking contributions; to Necy Fernandes for her assistance in my home and in my kitchens during the writing and photographing of this book; and to all the other members of my kitchen and office staff for their help.

Special thanks to Pat Guthman for letting me photograph in her Bee in the Kitchen shop and for use of antiques from the shop; to Debbie and Michael Lonsdale for permitting us to photograph at their charming home; to the Michael Friedman Gallery in Westport for the use of its wonderful antiques; to Celso Lima for his help in my garden; and to Laura Herbert, my sister, for the use of her pie plate collection.

Many thanks to Carolyn Hart Gavin for her supervision of the book at Clarkson N. Potter and her editing skills; to Gael Dillon, Carol Southern, Michael Fragnito, Sally Berk, Susan Magrino, and the rest of the Clarkson N. Potter and Crown Publishers staff; and to Kay Riley for her special help in pulling all the pieces together. Thanks to Henrietta Condak for her superb and imaginative design, and to her assistant Brenda Wolf for her perseverance and cheerfulness.

And finally, many thanks to all my readers who encourage me to write these books and support my efforts with their great enthusiasm and friendliness.

C O N T

E N T S

Introduction

WHEN I THINK OF PIES AND TARTS, I REMEMBER my childhood, when I was growing up on Elm Place in Nutley, New Jersey. We lived, the eight Kostyras, in a three-bedroom house set in a row of similar houses on a nice quiet street (quiet except for the voices of the many children who lived there). Each house was on a narrow plot measuring approximately 175 feet by 45 feet. My father loved to garden, so on our property there was very little lawn and lots of flowers, vegetables, fruit trees, and berry bushes. We had a magnificent McIntosh apple tree, which grew so large that Father cut it down in its prime, even though it provided us with bushels and bushels of perfect apples. The shade it cast over the flowers and other plants was too dense, he said.

Mr. and Mrs. Maus, our best friends, lived next door on an even smaller plot, but they grew wonderful berries and fruits, too. Retired bakers, they practiced their art almost daily, to the benefit of the whole neighborhood. In the center of their backyard grew a Montmorency cherry tree, and the pies they made of those wonderful sour cherries are among my most cherished memories. There was a white peach tree, too, which grew tall and irregularly over the Mauses' garage roof. I spent many hours in a crook of that tree, reading and listening from my hidden vantage point. I could hear almost everything that was said in our yard and in the yards of the Maus, Mendelson, Allegri, and Kastner families.

What made our suburban existence really special was a large fertile field behind our houses, part of an old farm. In the late 1940s and during the '50s we all planted extensive Victory gardens there. I was the only one of my father's children who took naturally to the garden—I never minded the hours in the blazing sun, weeding and cultivating. My father sent for every garden catalogue available, and we pored over them together, choosing what we would like to have on an imaginary estate, as well as what we could actually afford to have and take care of.

My mother spent most of her time in the kitchen, cooking, baking, and sewing. My time was spent outside in the garden; in the Mauses' flour-covered basement, learning how to make pie crust, kuchen doughs, yeast breads, and anything else they would show me; reading whatever I could get my hands on; and, of course, daydreaming in the peach tree. It occurred to me early on that gardening was very much like cooking. Both depended, at least in our neighborhood, on communication among people and a constant exchange of ideas and knowledge. The Mauses wanted me to know how to make the best cherry pie and the finest white peach tart. Mr. Allegri wanted me to know how he grew his beautiful holly trees, and every Sunday Mrs. Allegri showed me another of her meat-based sauces, which she served with an astonishing variety of homemade pasta.

Much later, when I had grown up, married, and moved to Westport, Connecticut, I met Fred Specht, an estate gardener who lived on the vast Von Rebay place, adjoining our two acres. Fred was so wise and taught me so much about gardening. He is retired now and lives on Cape Cod, but he visits us two or three times a year, and I am always delighted to see him.

Before we did anything else in Westport, Andy and I planted an orchard with apples, sour cherries, and white peaches, hoping to bring a bit of Nutley to our new home. My father worked long and hard with us in our gardens. He propagated cuttings of my favorite flowers and plants. He grew me a fig tree just like his. He sat with me while I planned the landscape, and by his patience, he taught me patience. I wanted our new garden to have the same easy, casual feeling that my childhood one had, only on a larger scale.

Our place in Westport grew as we needed more space for gardens. We bought the adjoining two acres, which were quickly absorbed into the master garden plan. Another two acres were added a couple of years ago, and we have exciting plans for a nuttery, a rhododendron garden, a woodland garden, and a maze, which Andy is designing. From our land in the Berkshires we brought back blueberry bushes and fruit trees that were in a low field being flooded by beavers. Middlefield, Massachusetts, is quite famous for its large, prolific blueberry bushes, and those bushes have thrived in Westport. Currant bushes were transplanted from the Von Rebay gardens, from slips that Fred gave me, and from a house nearby on the Post Road that was being demolished. We ordered quinces from the Leuthardt nursery on Long Island and fraises des bois from the White Flower Farm. Shiro plum trees and Chojuro pears were shipped from Miller's, and seven kinds of strawberries from Rayner's. My dentist traded me some of his grandmother's purple raspberry plants for a copy of *Quick Cook*™.

As Andy and I experimented with propagating fruits and berries, I experimented with them in new recipes, especially in pies and tarts. I discovered that currants make not only the clearest, reddest jelly, but a striking topping for an open-faced tart. I found out by mistake that sour cherries make not only fabulous pies but a delicate jelly. Quinces can be used to make a clear, pinkish-golden jelly, and also an unusual purée for apple tarts. I learned that certain apples are better than others for baking, for slicing, and for turning into sauces, and that certain pears are far superior to others for poaching or baking. And I found that white Belle of Georgia peaches really are as delicious in pies and tarts as I remember from my childhood.

Pies and tarts are ideal desserts. They are a combination of French, English, and American culinary tradition, and the recipes for them allow us to use all sorts of different ingredients. Good pies and tarts have a sweetness, tartness, and freshness that distinguish them from other kinds of desserts. They are simpler to make than the simplest cakes, and I like them even better.

I have tried to make most of the pies and tarts in this book quite easy. With very few exceptions, there are no complex fillings and no complicated mixtures of tastes and textures. When pies and tarts become too "busy" I like them less.

As for the crusts in which to put these wonderful pies and tarts, here, too, I have opted for simplicity and included only those crusts that are indispensable for pie and tart making.

This book contains all of my favorite pies and tarts, but it is not meant to be an encyclopedia of knowledge on the subject. My daughter Alexis is always telling me that *every* pie is my favorite—be it Mile-High Lemon Meringue Pie, Lemon Mousse Damask Tart, Chocolate Victoria Tartlets, or Pink Applesauce Primrose Tart—and that is probably true. I hope that this book will inspire my readers to love them, and enjoy making them, as much as I do.

GOLDEN RULES FOR PERFECT PIES AND TARTS

1. All ingredients for pastry must be ice-cold.

2. The pastry must be made very quickly. This is most easily accomplished by using a food processor, in which the entire mixing process should take no longer than 45 seconds.

3. Chill the pastry thoroughly before rolling it out.

4. Crusts should be rolled quickly, evenly, and with a minimum of flour. A soft-bristle brush can be used to remove excess flour.

5. Fruit pies must be baked in a hot, preheated oven to ensure well-done fruit, brown and flaky crusts, and thick juices. The juices in the center of the pie must bubble before the pie is actually done.

6. Completely bake pastry shells that are to be filled with a prepared filling. Partially bake shells when some or all of the filling is to be baked in the shell.

7. Fillings for pies and tarts are best when freshly prepared. Perfect fruit should be used, whether it is to be baked or used uncooked.

8. Glazes are to be used as adornment, not as cover-ups for inferior fillings.

A deeply ruffled heart-shaped crust holds a fluffy whipped cream filling topped with glistening ripe red currants.

CHAPTER 1.

THE MOST LOVED OF ALL PIES IN America is the old-fashioned apple pie. Its popularity has continued despite the unfortunate appearance in supermarkets of gooey commercial concoctions that look like apple pie but taste like rubber cement and contain barely a slice of apple. Homemade apple pie as we remember it, full of sweet-tart apple slices, flavored with sweet butter, cinnamon, and bits of lemon, is as easy to make as any pie in this book. We in the United States are fortunate in having consistently fine apples available most of the year. We don't have the varieties found in European markets, but we do have native apples that are excellent for eating and for baking and cooking. The crisp McIntosh, the green Granny Smith, the tart Cortland, the popular Yellow Delicious—all are fine for pies and tarts.

Andy and I have planted an orchard of 122 trees—large by ordinary suburban standards—in which we have experimented with many types of American and European apples. We have been very satisfied with most of the varieties, and found that all of them have unique qualities that make them attractive fruits to grow. Of course, not all of us have the opportunity or desire to grow numerous kinds of apple trees, and I don't urge everyone to have an orchard from which to pick Gravensteins or Winter Banana apples or Macouns or Black Gilliflowers. I've grown these apples because I had a professional and culinary interest in doing so. I've learned which are good for applesauce and apple butter, for pies, for tarts, for jelly. It's fun, and I have Andy to prune the trees.

All the pies and tarts in this chapter call for specific apples, because I have found that certain types work and taste better than others. But, of course, substitutions can be made, and I've given some suggestions for apples that might be more available in your area.

Apples

Tarte Tatin

There are many, many ways to bake a tarte tatin. I have had varying degrees of success with other methods, but this one seems to work best for me.

Tarte tatin is really an upside-down single-crust tart. The fruit is cooked in a butter-and-sugar mixture in a heavy-bottomed cast iron or tin-lined copper skillet, cooled slightly, covered with pâte brisée, and baked until the pastry is browned and the sugar and fruit juices are caramelized. After the tart has cooled for twenty or so minutes, it is reversed onto a serving platter. Because of the reversal, it is important to arrange the fruit decoratively and neatly while preparing the tart. For the traditional apple tarte tatin I use Cortlands, or Empire, or the very tasty Golden Delicious.

Clockwise from top left: *Apple, pear, and peach tarte tatins inverted onto silver serving platters. Early nineteenth-century handpainted canvas wallpaper covers the table.*

THE RECIPE

Makes one 9-inch tart

½ RECIPE PÂTE BRISÉE (PAGE 198), CHILLED

¾ CUP GRANULATED SUGAR
3 TABLESPOONS WATER

4 TABLESPOONS (½ STICK) UNSALTED BUTTER, CUT INTO SMALL PIECES
8 MEDIUM-SIZE TART CORTLAND APPLES

1. In an 8- or 9-inch cast iron skillet (or other ovenproof sauté pan), combine the sugar and water. Bring the mixture to a boil, lower the flame, and cook over medium heat until it begins to thicken and turn amber-colored. Remove from the heat and stir in the butter.

2. Halve and core the fruit. Leaving half an apple for the center of the tart, quarter the rest of the fruit and decoratively arrange the slices around the edge of the skillet on top of the caramelized sugar, cut sides up. (Remember that since the tarte tatin is inverted after it is cooked, the fruit on the bottom will be visible when served.) Place the apple half in the center. Continue layering in this fashion until the fruit is level with the top of the pan. If the fruit does not completely fill the pan, the tart will collapse when inverted.

3. Return the skillet to the stove and cook over low heat for about 20 minutes, until the syrup thickens and is reduced by half. Do not let the syrup burn. Remove from the heat and let cool.

4. Preheat the oven to 375°.

5. Roll out the pâte brisée to a thickness of ⅛ inch and place it over the apples. Trim the edges.

6. Bake the tart for about 20 minutes, until the pastry is golden brown. Let cool on a rack for 15 to 20 minutes, then loosen the pastry from the pan using a sharp knife. Place a serving dish or platter over the tart and quickly invert. Serve immediately.

VARIATIONS: Substitute pears (page 33) or peaches (page 47) for the apples. Peel the pears; peaches may be peeled or not, as desired.

Apple Croustade

In Paris while I was buying baking equipment for this book, I came across a five-volume work by the great French pâtissier-chef Yves Thuries, *Le Livre de Recettes d'un Compagnon du Tour de France* (1979), which has greatly influenced the making and baking of classic desserts in France and elsewhere. I especially like the croustades he describes—fruit tarts made from two rounds of thinly rolled puff pastry, sealed and decorated with leaves or strips of leftover pastry. These croustades are very pretty and can be filled with apples, pears, cherries, or plums. Before baking, the top is glazed with a simple egg-water mixture and sprinkled with granulated sugar. Baked in a 400° oven, the pastry puffs and turns a rich golden brown, while the fruit filling becomes tender and juicy. If the edges are well sealed, the juices do not ooze from the croustade.

The decorative leaves on this puff pastry tart were affixed with ice water before glazing and baking.

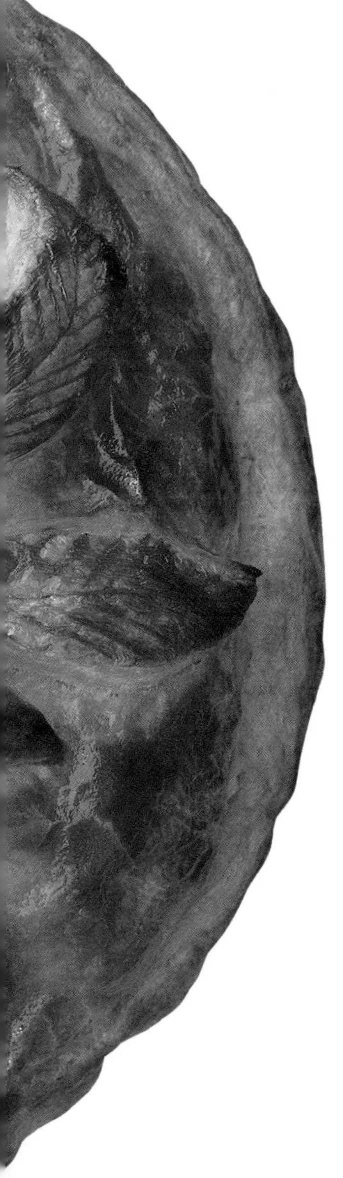

T H E R E C I P E

Makes one 12-inch double-crust tart

1 POUND PUFF PASTRY (PAGE 206)

- **4 TART GRANNY SMITH OR CRITERION APPLES, PEELED, CORED, AND VERY THINLY SLICED**
- **3 TABLESPOONS GRANULATED SUGAR**
- **1 TABLESPOON ALL-PURPOSE FLOUR**
- **GRATED RIND OF 1 LEMON**
- **¼ TEASPOON FRESHLY GRATED NUTMEG**
- **2 TABLESPOONS COLD UNSALTED BUTTER, CUT INTO SMALL PIECES**

GLAZE: 1 EGG BEATEN WITH 2 TEASPOONS WATER
GRANULATED SUGAR

1. Roll out the pastry to a thickness of no more than ⅛ inch. Using cake pans or circles of cardboard as a guide, cut one 12-inch circle and one 11-inch circle from the pastry. With a sharp paring knife, cut out as many leaf shapes as possible from the scraps. Make veins in each with the back of the knife. Place the circles and leaves on a parchment-lined or water-sprayed baking sheet, cover with plastic wrap, and refrigerate for at least 30 minutes.

2. To make the filling, combine the apples, sugar, flour, lemon rind, and nutmeg in a large mixing bowl and stir well. Set aside.

3. Preheat the oven to 400°.

4. To make the tart, place the 12-inch circle of puff pastry on a parchment-lined or water-sprayed baking sheet. Spoon the filling onto the center of the pastry and spread it out evenly to within 1½ inches of the edge. Dot with butter. Center the 11-inch circle on top. Moisten the edges of the pastry with water, bring up the ½-inch border from the bottom pastry, fold it over, and press to seal. Using ice water, paste the leaves on top of the tart. Brush the pastry lightly with the glaze and sprinkle with sugar. Bake for approximately 50 to 60 minutes, until puffed and golden brown. Let cool on a rack before serving.

Winter Banana Apple Tart

This is possibly one of the most beautiful of all apple tarts, made from a rather obscure apple—the Winter Banana or Banana Delicious apple. The flavor is delicate, the texture meltingly smooth. I don't know why they are named Banana apples, and the few growers I contacted didn't know either. They are a novelty apple with very creamy, tender flesh and skin of the palest creamy yellow blushed with rosy pink, as shown in the photograph.

This unusual fluted-edge tart glistens on a simple clear glass pedestal plate.

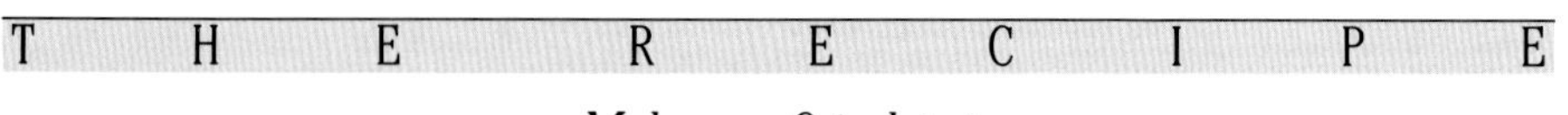

THE RECIPE

Makes one 9-inch tart

ONE 9-INCH PÂTE BRISÉE TART SHELL (PAGE 198), PARTIALLY BAKED AND COOLED

8 OR 9 MEDIUM-SIZE WINTER BANANA APPLES, PEELED, CORED, AND SLICED LENGTHWISE VERY THINLY

⅓ CUP CALVADOS OR APPLE BRANDY

⅓ CUP GRANULATED SUGAR

½ CUP QUINCE OR SOUR CHERRY GLAZE (PAGE 211)

1. Preheat the oven to 350°.

2. Put half the apple slices in a shallow dish. Pour the Calvados over the apples and let them macerate for 30 minutes.

3. Drain the slices and arrange them in neat overlapping circular rows in the partially baked tart shell. Sprinkle with the sugar and bake for approximately 20 minutes, until the apples are soft. Remove the tart from the oven and arrange the remaining apple slices in a spiral over the cooked apples. Return it to the oven and bake for 5 minutes longer.

4. Turn the oven to broil. Brush the apples and crust edges with the jelly glaze and leave the tart under the broiler until the glaze becomes shiny and the edges of crust and apples darken. Serve the tart immediately or let it cool slightly.

APPLES

On a recent trip to France to visit my daughter Alexis while she completed her summer employment, I discovered this petal-shaped tart form at Dehillerin and bought it, along with other forms difficult to find in the United States. I had no plans for the petal form until one day when I made some bright pink applesauce from some very red-skinned McIntosh apples. I thought the color especially reminiscent of early pink primroses that bloom in damp woods. It was quite a coincidence when we took the tart to Pat Guthman's Bee in the Kitchen antiques shop in Southport, Connecticut, to find a whole creamware tea service in a pattern called New England Primrose, c. 1810. We also located pink damask fringed napkins, and photographed the tart as you see it.

As with several of the apple tarts in this book, I did not peel the apples, preferring instead the bright color and design of unpeeled fruit. Because the apples are so thin, a few minutes of baking softens them so that they are very tender and can be cut with a dessert fork.

Pale pink sour cherry glaze coats this lovely tart and gives it an even pinker glow.

Pink Applesauce Primrose Tart

THE RECIPE

Makes one 10½-inch tart

ONE 10½-INCH PÂTE BRISÉE TART SHELL (PAGE 198), BAKED AND COOLED

4 TABLESPOONS (½ STICK) UNSALTED BUTTER

2 TABLESPOONS CALVADOS OR COGNAC

¼ CUP GRANULATED SUGAR

3½ CUPS UNSWEETENED APPLESAUCE, PREFERABLY HOMEMADE FROM UNPEELED RED-SKINNED APPLES (SEE NOTE BELOW)

2 TO 3 FIRM TART RED-SKINNED MCINTOSH APPLES

¼ CUP SOUR CHERRY GLAZE (PAGE 211)

1. Preheat the oven to 400°.

2. To make the filling, melt the butter, Calvados, and sugar in a medium saucepan over low heat, stirring until the sugar is dissolved. Add the applesauce and heat through.

3. Core the apples and slice them crosswise as thinly as possible using an electric meat slicer or a very sharp knife. Put the applesauce filling in the tart shell and neatly arrange the apple slices on top, following the shape of the tart ring and overlapping the slices. Bake for approximately 10 minutes, to soften the apples.

4. Immediately before serving, turn the oven to broil. Lightly brush the apple slices with the sour cherry glaze and place under the broiler for 2 to 3 minutes, or just until the glaze melts and the edges of the apples darken.

NOTE: To make applesauce, quarter the apples—do not peel them—and remove the seeds. Cook in a small amount of water until they become soft and mushy. Let the apples cool slightly and put them through a food mill. If you have used bright red-skinned apples, as we did, your applesauce should be a lovely pink color. (Ten medium-size apples yield approximately 4 cups of applesauce.)

Apple Petal Tart

This is a variation of the Winter Banana Apple Tart (page 12), which was baked in a round tart pan. I very much like the petal-shaped tart "rings" that I purchased in Paris at Dehillerin. This unusual shape comes in several sizes and two heights: one for shallow tarts, like the Pink Applesauce Primrose Tart (page 15), and this deeper version, which is excellent for tarts with more filling. Because of the depth of this tart, ten to twelve apples (we used Golden Pippins and Criterions) were thinly sliced and baked in this petal form.

For this tart I arranged layers of apple slices around the perimeter and then filled the center of the "flower" with more apples.

Apple Galette

This tart is a variation of the Nectarine Galette, or open-faced fruit puff pastry tart, described on page 58. I used two Golden Pippin apples. When baked, they became almost transparent, with only the edges darkened by the high oven temperature. One 9-inch galette serves two generously, or four more modestly.

An apple galette for two is cut into four wedges and served with dollops of whipped cream on pale green Depression glass dessert plates.

Apple Butter Tartlets

Each autumn Andy and I are faced with a dilemma—what to do with all the odd leftover apples from the apple trees we've planted. There are bushels of drops after a windy night or a heavy rain, as well as bruised apples, a few wormy ones, and just the general overflow that a small family such as ours could never eat. Apple butter for canning and applesauce for freezing are my two favorite uses for them.

My favorite apple butter begins with fresh apple purée, preferably from a mélange of varieties—the red-striped Gold Parmain, very dark red Black Gilliflower, orange Cox, snowy-white red-skinned Fameuse, Grimes Golden, and crisp Gravenstein. I put up this butter in pint and half-pint jars, and use it all winter in tarts, on toast, and in applesauce spice cakes. It is one of my favorite preserves to include in the Christmas baskets we make each year for corporate clients. Homemade apple butter has no equal! (Except possibly homemade peach, plum, or pear butter, made in a similar fashion but with slightly different spices.)

We make apple butter tartlets no larger than 4 inches in diameter, and often smaller, for use as finger desserts.

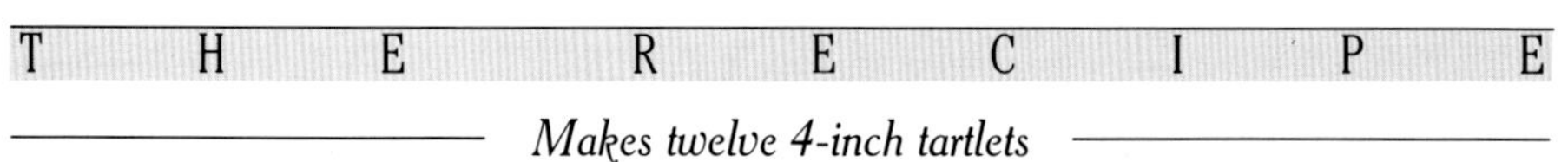

Makes twelve 4-inch tartlets

TWELVE 4-INCH PÂTE BRISÉE TARTLET SHELLS (PAGE 198), PARTIALLY BAKED AND COOLED

Apple Butter

Makes 1 quart

- **4 CUPS FRESH APPLE PURÉE OR UNSWEETENED APPLESAUCE (SEE NOTE, PAGE 15)**
- **1½ CUPS PACKED DARK BROWN SUGAR**
- **1 TEASPOON CINNAMON**
- **¼ TEASPOON ALLSPICE**
- **PINCH OF GROUND CLOVES**
- **JUICE AND GRATED RIND OF 1 LEMON**

- **6 FIRM TART CORTLAND APPLES, PEELED, CORED, AND THINLY SLICED**
- **1 TEASPOON CINNAMON MIXED WITH 2 TABLESPOONS GRANULATED SUGAR**
- **1 CUP DARK OR GOLDEN RAISINS, SOAKED OVERNIGHT IN 2 TABLESPOONS COGNAC (OPTIONAL)**

1. To make the apple butter, combine all ingredients in a heavy saucepan and cook over low heat for approximately 4 hours, until the mixture is thick and dark brown. Take care not to scorch the butter. Remove from the stove and let cool.

2. Preheat the oven to 375°.

3. To make the tartlets, spoon approximately ¼ cup of apple butter into each tartlet shell, top with several apple slices, and sprinkle with a bit of cinnamon sugar or Cognac-soaked raisins, if desired. Bake for 10 to 15 minutes, just until the apples soften. Serve warm.

When making lots of these apple butter tartlets, I like to vary the flavor and design of the toppings.

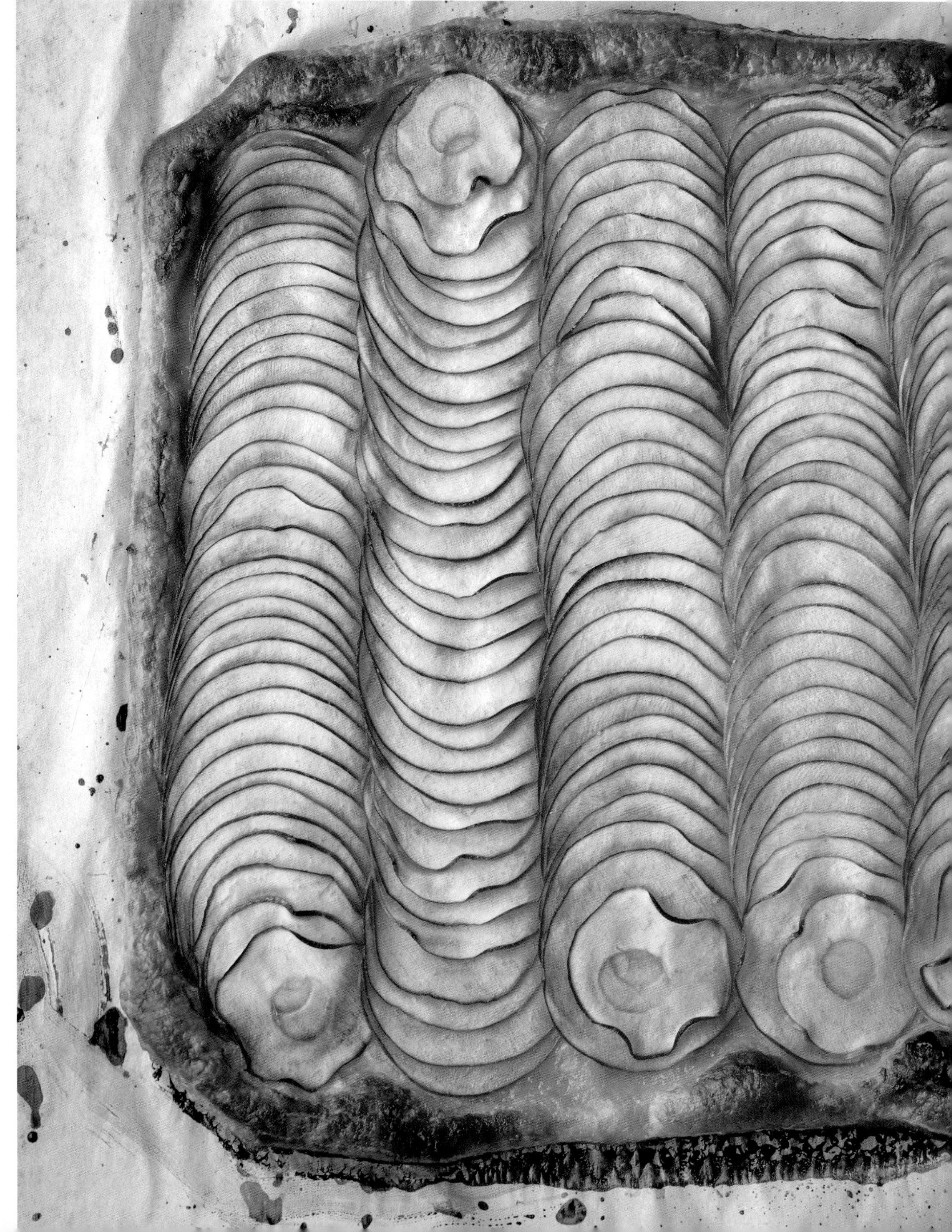

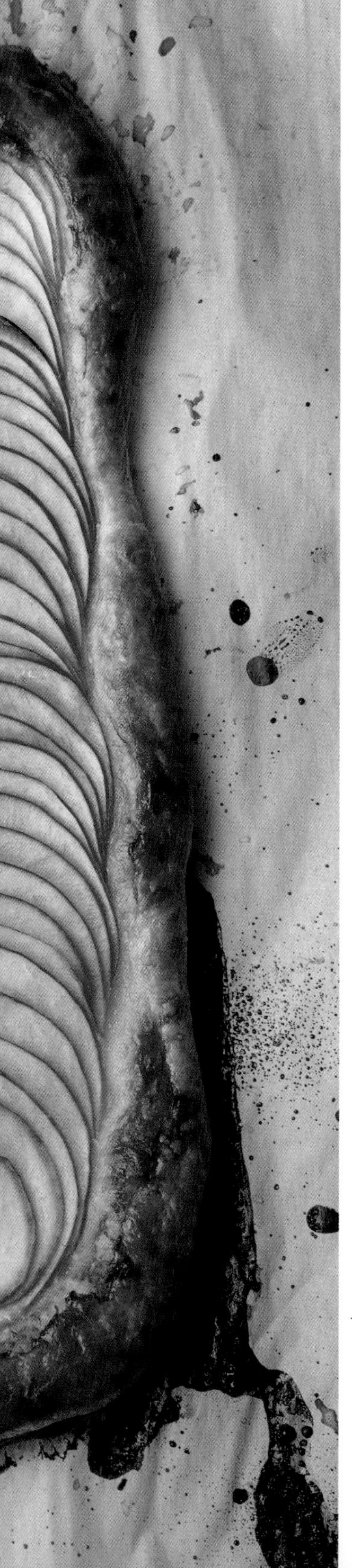

Paper-thin slices of apple are arranged in rows on top of an irregularly shaped square of puff pastry. You could roll out the pastry for this tart in any shape you like—oval, triangle, circle, or square, either large or small.

Years ago, I tasted my first free-form puff pastry apple tart at Eli Zabar's E.A.T. on Madison Avenue. It was made with peeled Yellow Delicious apples and glazed with an extract of apple cider. The combination of the delicate puff pastry and the fresh flavor of thinly sliced apple was wonderful.

I made this version using unpeeled red-skinned Gravenstein apples from our one Gravenstein tree, a small amount of sugar, and a sprinkling of Sauternes. I like this tart with no glaze at all, and serve it with softly whipped crème fraîche.

THE RECIPE

Makes one 12 × 12-inch tart

1 POUND PUFF PASTRY (PAGE 206)

5 TABLESPOONS GRANULATED SUGAR
5 OR 6 FIRM TART GRAVENSTEIN APPLES
¼ CUP SWEET WHITE WINE, PREFERABLY SAUTERNES

GARNISH: CRÈME FRAÎCHE (OPTIONAL)

1. Preheat the oven to 400°.
2. Roll out the puff pastry to a large square approximately ⅛ inch thick. Turn the edges up just slightly to form a lip. Sprinkle 1 tablespoon sugar evenly over the crust, transfer the pastry to a parchment-lined or water-sprayed baking sheet, cover with plastic wrap, and refrigerate.
3. Core the apples and slice them crosswise as thinly as possible—1/16 inch is desirable. (We used an electric meat slicer for this job.) Lay the apple slices out on the pastry in overlapping rows and brush with the wine. Sprinkle the remaining sugar over the apples, and bake for approximately 30 to 35 minutes, until the pastry edges are browned. If the tart hasn't browned sufficiently, put it under the broiler for a minute or so. Watch carefully to prevent burning. Let cool before cutting. Garnish with softly whipped crème fraîche, if desired.

VARIATION: The tart can also be glazed after baking with a clear jelly glaze—crab apple, quince, or sour cherry (page 211).

My sister Laura Herbert collects antique pie plates, the kind that years ago were sold with pies for a 10¢ deposit. When she wants to bake a pie, she simply removes one of the tins from her wall display.

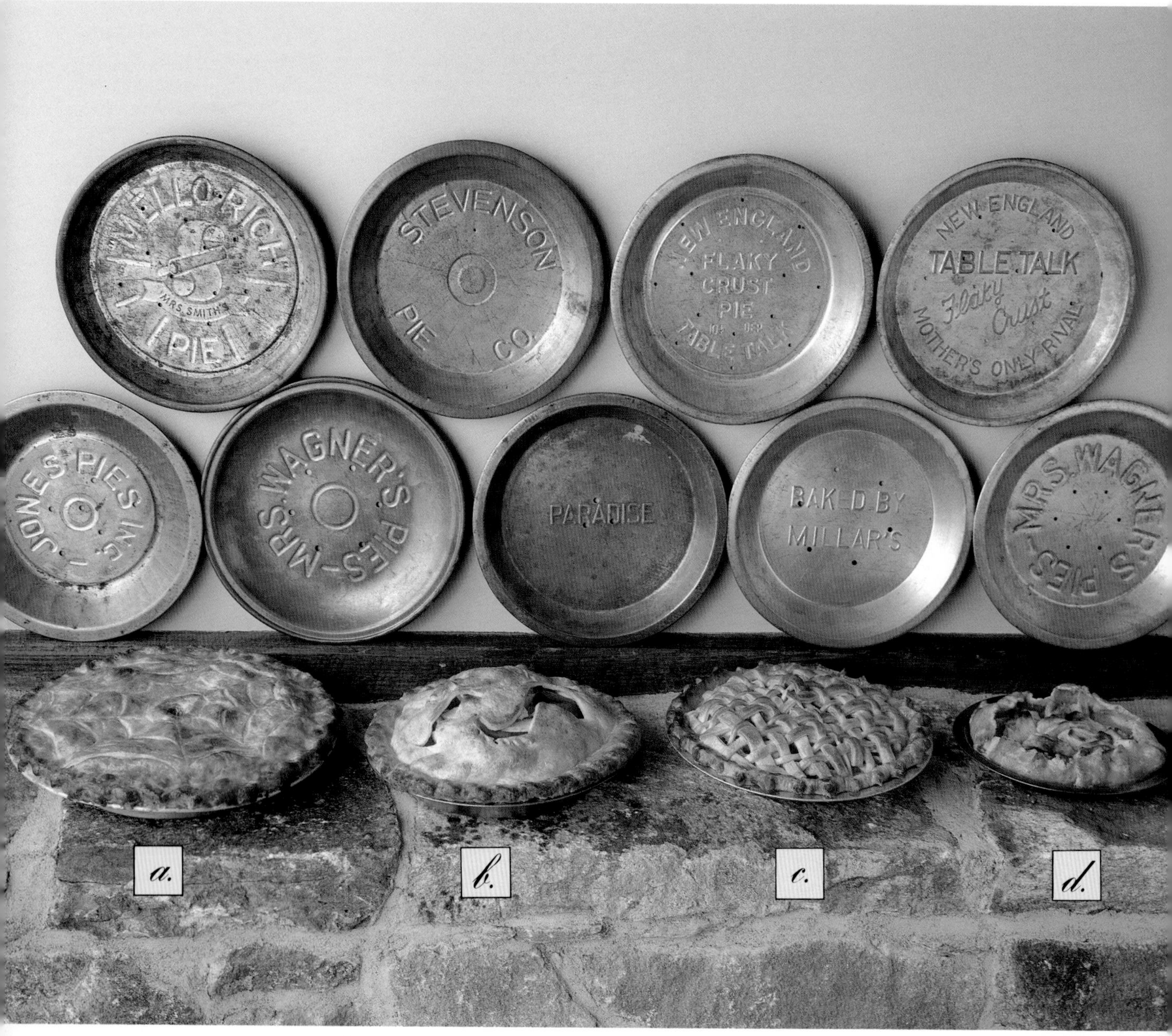

a.

b.

c.

d.

a Spiderweb Apple Pie

We have a cottage in the heart of the Berkshires, in Middlefield, Massachusetts. Every August, a real, old-fashioned country fair is held. For the twenty years we have been attending this fair, the same resident of Middlefield has walked off with all the blue ribbons for her home-baked pies. Mrs. Horalek, when questioned, admits that her crust is always made with lard or Crisco, never with butter or margarine. Another fine pie baker, Carol Varsano, always uses margarine in her crust, which is so tender it crumbles when cut and melts in your mouth.

This spiderweb apple pie, made with Cortland apples, uses crust made with solid vegetable shortening or lard. It looks like Mrs. Horalek's, and I hope it is as tender and flaky. The filling is just apples with a little lemon, cinnamon, nutmeg, and cloves. We sprinkled a bit of flour into the filling, because there can be quite a lot of juice when twelve to fourteen apples are baked in a crust. The flour helps thicken the juice so that the bottom crust does not become soggy. No glaze was used on this pie, but a bit of milk can be brushed on before baking for a deeper color, if you prefer.

THE RECIPE

Makes one 10-inch double-crust pie

TWO 10-INCH CIRCLES OF NON-BUTTER CRUST (PAGE 203), CHILLED

12 TO 14 TART CORTLAND APPLES, PEELED, CORED, AND SLICED
3 TABLESPOONS ALL-PURPOSE FLOUR
⅔ CUP GRANULATED SUGAR
SCANT ½ TEASPOON EACH CINNAMON AND NUTMEG
PINCH OF GROUND CLOVES
GRATED RIND AND JUICE OF 1 LEMON
2 TABLESPOONS COLD UNSALTED BUTTER, CUT INTO SMALL PIECES

1. Preheat the oven to 400°.

2. Press one pastry circle into a 10-inch pie plate. Place the other circle on wax paper and, using a kitchen knife or the back of a paring knife, make a "spiderweb" design on top of the pastry. Do *not* cut through the pastry. Cut out a small hole in the center of the top crust as a steam vent. Cover both crusts with plastic wrap so the pastry doesn't dry out, and chill.

3. Put the sliced apples in a large mixing bowl, add the flour, sugar, spices, and lemon rind and juice, and mix. Turn the apples into the chilled pastry, dot with butter, and cover with the pastry top. Seal and crimp the edges as desired.

4. Bake the pie for approximately 45 minutes, or until the crust is browned and the juices are bubbling inside. Let cool before serving.

6. Apple-Raisin Pie

While preparing the pies for this book, we baked in tin, glass, crockery, and aluminum pie dishes. The best crusts were achieved when we baked in the old-fashioned, inexpensive lightweight tin pie plates. All the fruit pies had brown, crisp bottom crusts, and the crimped and decorated edges retained their designs well. The overall color of top and bottom crusts was uniform and golden brown.

This apple-raisin pie, in keeping with our desire to bake uncomplicated pies, is simple —just apples, raisins, Cognac, a bit of sugar and butter. It is a two-crust pie, homey in appearance, vented with large S cuts in the top crust and heavily crimped edges. Because the pâte brisée is so buttery and flaky, I rarely cut all the excess pastry away from the edges of a fruit pie. I prefer to trim it so that the overhang is even, then fold or roll it up to make a thick edge. Crimping can be by any of the methods illustrated on page 204. No one will leave the pastry edges uneaten!

A closer look at one of Laura's wonderful antique pie plates. She likes to collect only ones that have names or sayings on them. Small holes in the bottoms of these tins help make the bottom crust crisper.

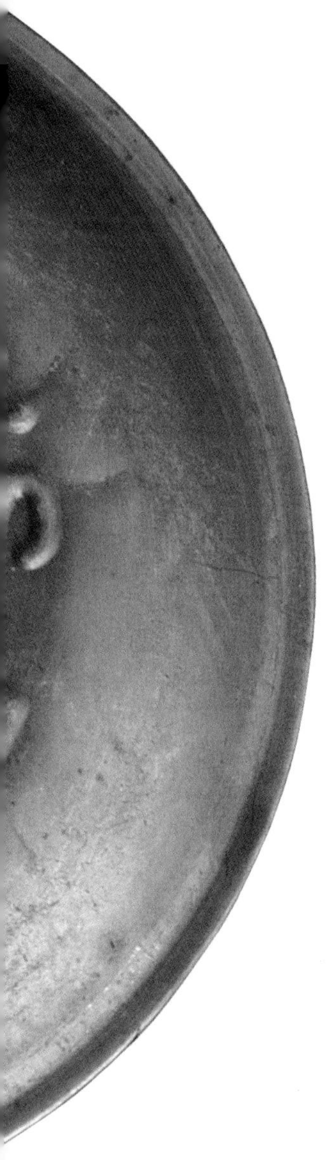

T H E R E C I P E

Makes one 8-inch double-crust pie

PÂTE BRISÉE (PAGE 198) FOR A DOUBLE-CRUST 8-INCH PIE, CHILLED

- **9 MEDIUM-SIZE FIRM TART APPLES (WE USED A COMBINATION OF WINTER BANANA AND MCINTOSH), PEELED, CORED, AND THINLY SLICED**
- **½ CUP RAISINS, SOAKED OVERNIGHT IN 2 TABLESPOONS COGNAC**
- **⅓ CUP GRANULATED SUGAR**
- **2 TABLESPOONS COLD UNSALTED BUTTER, CUT INTO SMALL PIECES**

1. Preheat the oven to 400°.

2. Roll out half the pastry to a thickness of ⅛ inch, press into an 8-inch pie plate, and chill. Roll out the remaining pastry and with a very sharp knife make several S-shaped vents in the center. Place the top pastry on a parchment-lined or water-sprayed baking sheet, or on wax paper, and chill.

3. Put the apple slices and raisins in a mixing bowl, sprinkle with sugar, and toss to mix well. Pour this mixture into the chilled bottom crust and dot with butter. Carefully cover the apples with the top pastry, trim the overhang, and crimp the edges to seal.

4. Bake the pie for 45 to 50 minutes, or until the pastry is nicely browned and the juices in the center of the pie are bubbling. Let cool slightly on a wire rack before serving.

Latticework Apple Pie

We used tart, crispy Macouns to make this lattice-covered pie, which is a little different from plain apple pies because of the coriander, allspice, and grated orange rind. McIntosh apples could be substituted. They are a bit softer than Macouns and cook faster, so I usually cut them into larger chunks.

The lattice was woven right on top of the pie filling. It is only when the filling is wet or warm that the lattice must be woven on a sheet of wax paper or parchment and transferred to the top of the pie in one quick step (see the Chocolate Pecan Lattice Tart, page 172).

THE RECIPE

Makes one 9-inch double-crust pie

ONE 9-INCH CIRCLE OF PÂTE BRISÉE (PAGE 198), PLUS EXTRA PASTRY FOR THE LATTICE TOP, CHILLED

8 TO 9 MEDIUM-SIZE TART MACOUN APPLES, PEELED, CORED, AND SLICED
¼ TEASPOON GROUND CORIANDER
¼ TEASPOON ALLSPICE
GRATED RIND OF 1 LARGE ORANGE
1 TABLESPOON ALL-PURPOSE FLOUR
½ CUP GRANULATED SUGAR
3 TABLESPOONS COLD UNSALTED BUTTER, CUT INTO SMALL PIECES

1. Preheat the oven to 400°.

2. Press the pastry circle into a 9-inch pie plate. Roll out the remaining pastry to a thickness of no more than ⅛ inch and cut it into as many lattice strips as possible. (We varied the width of the strips and used ¼-inch strips horizontally and ½-inch strips vertically.) Chill all pastry, covered, until ready to use.

3. In a mixing bowl, mix the apples with the spices, orange rind, flour, and sugar, being sure to coat the slices thoroughly. Turn the mixture into the prepared bottom crust and dot with butter. Weave the lattice strips over the filling and secure the ends by pasting them to the crust with a bit of water. Crimp the edges to seal and bake for 50 to 60 minutes, until the crust is nicely browned and the juices in the center of the pie are bubbling. Let cool slightly before serving.

d. Bottom-Crust Apple Pie

This is perhaps the easiest pie to make in this book. All you need is a round of pastry 14 inches in diameter, eight tasty apples, a bit of sugar, butter, and a few spices. I keep rounds of pastry rolled out and frozen between sheets of plastic wrap so that I can make pies like this with just a few moments' preparation. The pastry needs approximately five minutes to thaw enough to be pressed into the bottom of a pie tin. The edges are left untrimmed and are folded over the filling.

This type of pie can be made with many other fruits—plums, peaches, pears, cherries, rhubarb, etc. Flavorings may vary with the type of fruit used. Remember, it is the fresh fruit that makes this pie so delicious, and the simpler the ingredients the better the pie.

THE RECIPE

Makes one 8-inch pie

ONE 14-INCH CIRCLE OF PÂTE BRISÉE (PAGE 198), CHILLED

- **8 FIRM TART MCINTOSH OR CORTLAND APPLES, PEELED, CORED, AND THINLY SLICED**
- **½ CUP GRANULATED SUGAR**
- **1 TEASPOON CINNAMON**
- **PINCH OF GROUND MACE**
- **PINCH OF FRESHLY GRATED NUTMEG**
- **2 TABLESPOONS COLD UNSALTED BUTTER, CUT INTO SMALL PIECES**

1. Preheat the oven to 375°.

2. Center the round of pastry in an 8-inch pie plate, pressing it into the corners. Place the apple slices in the pastry and sprinkle with the sugar and spices. Dot with butter. Bring the pastry overhang up over the apples. Bake for approximately 45 minutes, or until the crust is golden brown and the filling bubbly. Let cool slightly and gently slide the pie from the baking tin onto a serving dish. The top of the pie can be lightly dusted with confectioners' sugar, if desired.

VARIATION: This pie is delicious topped with a thick sprinkling of oatmeal–brown sugar crumbs. It is a bit more complicated but very, very good. Trim the pastry overhang and crimp the edges before topping with crumbs.

Crumb Topping

For one 8-inch pie

- **½ CUP (1 STICK) COLD UNSALTED BUTTER, CUT INTO ¼-INCH PIECES**
- **½ CUP ALL-PURPOSE FLOUR**
- **¾ CUP PACKED DARK BROWN SUGAR**
- **1 CUP ROLLED OATS**

In a food processor, quickly cut the butter into the flour until the mixture resembles oatmeal. (Of course, this can be done with your fingers, two knives, or a pastry cutter.) Mix in the sugar and oats and spoon over the fruit filling. Bake as directed above.

CHAPTER 2.

WE ARE FORTUNATE THAT PEARS, AS well as apples, peaches, and other fruits, are being grown in greater numbers and varieties than ever before. Six or seven excellent varieties are available from October through June in this country. The more common of these, including Red and Yellow Bartletts, have extended growing periods and can be found in supermarkets most of the year.

I will often make simple pear pies or sugar-crust tarts when I have four or five perfect pears on hand. Most pears we buy are not ripe—they are often picked hard because of their tendency to bruise severely. Pears should be ripened at home, on a windowsill, in a bowl or basket. (The presence of a banana can help speed up the process.) Because pears ripen from the inside out, it is hard to tell when a pear is ready to eat. The skin will yield to gentle pressure, and, of course, there should be a fragrance that will tell you the fruit is edible.

A perfectly ripe pear is buttery, not too soft, juicy, and mellow, with a depth of flavor that is peculiar to pears. It is wonderful to savor this complexity of taste, and to compare the very different flavors of different pears. Comice, Anjou, Bosc, Packham, Bartlett, Chojuro, and Forelle pears are all wonderful for eating and for poaching, baking, and cooking. Some are delicious as sorbet, too, and even in salad.

I've called for specific types of pears in this chapter because I have discovered that these pears are tastiest for particular recipes. However, as with the apple pie and tart recipes, substitutions are often fine.

Pears

Puff Pear Croustade with Anise

This is another of Yves Thuries's elegant croustades, from his excellent five-volume work on pastry (see page 11 for the Apple Croustade): a pear filling encased in two thin rounds of puff pastry, sealed and decorated in this instance with long strips of pastry. For this croustade I used Comice pears, which are large and round with buttery, aromatic flesh. Yellow Bartletts, Red Bartletts, and Packham pears are also excellent for croustades, because they are tender and bake as quickly as the pastry. Harder pears, such as Bosc and Anjou, might remain underdone in such a double-crust tart.

Making this type of croustade is relatively simple. Plain pâte brisée can be used, but I prefer puff pastry, for it is lighter, flakier, and more delicate. The combination of pear slices, grated orange rind, and aniseed makes this tart very special. The small bit of flour that is mixed into the filling acts as a thickener for the juices; without it, the fruit is too watery for the pastry. This dessert can be served alone or with crème fraîche or sweetened heavy cream.

T H E R E C I P E

Makes one 12-inch double-crust tart

1 POUND PUFF PASTRY (PAGE 206), CHILLED

9 SMALL, RIPE COMICE PEARS
⅓ CUP GRANULATED SUGAR
1 TEASPOON GRATED ORANGE RIND
SCANT ¼ TEASPOON ANISEED
1 TABLESPOON ALL-PURPOSE FLOUR

GLAZE: 1 EGG BEATEN WITH 2 TEASPOONS WATER
GRANULATED SUGAR

GARNISH: CRÈME FRAÎCHE OR SWEETENED HEAVY CREAM (OPTIONAL)

1. Roll out the pastry and cut two circles as described for the Apple Croustade (page 11). Using a pastry wheel, cut long ½-inch-wide strips from the scraps. Place the circles and strips on a parchment-lined or water-sprayed baking sheet and chill, covered, for at least 30 minutes.

2. To make the filling, peel and core the pears and slice them lengthwise. Put them in a large mixing bowl, add the remaining ingredients, and toss well. Set aside.

3. Preheat the oven to 400°.

4. To make the tart, place the 12-inch circle of puff pastry on a parchment-lined or water-sprayed baking sheet. Spoon the filling onto the center of the pastry and spread it out evenly to within 1½ inches of the edge. Center the 11-inch circle on top. Moisten the edges of the pastry with water, bring up the ½-inch border from the bottom pastry, fold it over, and press to seal. Using ice water, paste the ½-inch trimmings on top of the tart in a decorative pattern. Brush the pastry lightly with the glaze and sprinkle with sugar. Bake for approximately 50 to 60 minutes, until puffed and golden brown. Let cool on a rack before serving. Garnish with softly whipped crème fraîche or sweetened heavy cream, if desired.

At left: *A tender pear croustade is served in the shade of our orchard atop an old tavern table. Lemon tea, served in Fire King cups, is a perfect accompaniment.*

Red Bartletts in Cream

For *Quick Cook*™ I devised a recipe for pears baked in cream, which at the time seemed the simplest, most delicious of pear desserts. This recipe is not really more complicated, and I think it is even better. The crust, baked until crunchy and dark golden brown, tastes like a sugar cookie, and the pear juices and cream become custardlike.

Many people complain about the difficulty of rolling sweet pastry into a round that will not tear or crack. But because sweet pastry is soft, it can be easily pressed into the pan, like cookie dough, to mend any cracks. In any event, the crust for this tart need not be perfect to be delicious.

T H E R E C I P E

Makes one 12-inch tart

ONE 12-INCH CIRCLE OF PÂTE SUCRÉE EXTRA (PAGE 202), WELL CHILLED

5 FIRM BUT RIPE RED BARTLETT PEARS

3 TABLESPOONS UNSALTED BUTTER, AT ROOM TEMPERATURE

⅓ CUP VANILLA SUGAR (SEE NOTE, PAGE 55)

1 CUP HEAVY CREAM

1. Preheat the oven to 400°.

2. Roll out the pastry to a thickness of ¼ inch, carefully place it in a 12-inch tart pan, and crimp the edges as desired. If the pastry tears, gently press it back together. Chill.

3. Halve and core the pears, but do not peel them. Rub the skins with butter and arrange the pear halves, cut side down, in the prepared tart shell. Sprinkle with vanilla sugar and bake for 15 to 20 minutes, or until the pears begin to soften. Pour the cream around the pears, return the tart to the oven, and bake for another 10 to 15 minutes. Serve warm.

At left: *Halves of Bartlett pears are arranged in a crunchy cookie-like crust, sprinkled with vanilla sugar, and surrounded with cream.*

Pear Tarte Tatin

More than any of the other pear recipes, this tart emphasizes the finest qualities of the fruit. The buttery texture, the mellow sweet flavor, and the perfection of form and shape of the pear are exaggerated to the fullest.

Pears go very well with many other flavors, including ginger, chocolate, red and white wines, port and sherry, and almonds. They go especially well with caramel, and the delicate caramel flavor of this upside-down single-crust tart is really special. I like to serve it at room temperature or slightly warm, with huge dollops of heavy cream whipped with a bit of caramel syrup.

Follow the recipe for Tarte Tatin on page 9, substituting six to eight peeled Anjou or Bartlett pears for the apples.

The pale golden color of Anjou pears in a flaky pâte brisée crust makes this tart one of the loveliest.

Red & White Pear Tart

This very long rectangular tart of alternating red and white wine poached pears was invented at the last minute before a dinner party two years ago. I liked the result so much that I've made it many times since. I poached Bosc pears in a red wine and cassis syrup and Bartlett pears in a lemony white wine syrup. The pears were cooked whole, with the stems intact. For a 21-inch-long tart, you need three of each type of pear, halved lengthwise. (Leftover poached pears will keep for several days in the refrigerator. They taste wonderful served with crème anglaise (page 167) or even just whipped cream.)

The pears are placed in a baked tart shell, cut sides down, alternating color and direction. A simple egg and cream custard, which can be flavored with pear liqueur if desired, is spooned around the pears, and the tart is baked until the custard is set.

For serving, it is nice to cut the tart into narrow strips and serve each guest one red and one white pear.

I baked this tart on a heavy rolled steel baking sheet, because it doesn't buckle when placed in a hot oven, and it helps long rectangular tarts like this retain their shape.

T H E R E C I P E

Makes one large rectangular tart

ONE 4½ × 21 × 1-INCH PÂTE SUCRÉE TART SHELL (PAGE 202), BAKED AND COOLED

Red Wine Poached Pears

1 BOTTLE OF DRY RED WINE
1 STAR ANISE
1 JUNIPER BERRY
⅓ CUP CRÈME DE CASSIS
ZEST OF 1 BRIGHT-SKINNED ORANGE
2 WHOLE CLOVES
¼ CUP GRANULATED SUGAR
5 FIRM BUT RIPE BOSC PEARS, WITH STEMS LEFT ON, PEELED

White Wine Poached Pears

1 BOTTLE OF CHAMPAGNE, SPARKLING WHITE WINE, OR DRY WHITE WINE
2 TABLESPOONS FRESHLY SQUEEZED LEMON JUICE
1 CUP GRANULATED SUGAR
1 CINNAMON STICK
ZEST OF 1 LEMON
½ VANILLA BEAN
5 FIRM BUT RIPE BARTLETT PEARS, WITH STEMS LEFT ON, PEELED

Custard

2 EGGS
½ CUP GRANULATED SUGAR
⅓ CUP SIFTED ALL-PURPOSE FLOUR
1 CUP HEAVY CREAM
4 TABLESPOONS PEAR LIQUEUR (OPTIONAL)

CONFECTIONERS' SUGAR

1. Poach the pears in red and white wine, using the same method: Combine all ingredients, except the pears, in a large saucepan. Bring the mixture to a boil and cook for 5 minutes. Add the pears, lower the heat, and cook for 20 to 30 minutes, until the pears are tender. If necessary, turn the pears very gently by rotating the stems with your fingertips so that they cook evenly. Remove the pears to a bowl, bring the poaching liquid to a rapid boil, and reduce by half. Pour the syrup over the pears and refrigerate, covered, for at least 6 hours, preferably overnight.

2. To make the custard, beat the eggs and sugar until thick and pale yellow. Add the flour, mixing well. Add the cream and liqueur and beat until smooth.

3. Preheat the oven to 400°.

4. To make the tart, halve and carefully core the cooled poached pears, being careful to leave the stems intact. Choose the 5 most perfect halves and place them on the pastry, alternating the color and direction of each. (Depending on the tart frame you use, you may need a different number of pears.) Pour the custard evenly into the baked tart shell around the bottom of the pears (use just enough to come halfway up the pears). Bake for 20 to 25 minutes, or until the custard is set and lightly golden. Remove from the oven, dust with confectioners' sugar, and bake for 5 to 10 minutes more, just until the sugar melts. Serve warm.

STANFORD

Pear Frangipane Tart

T H E R E C I P E

Makes one 10-inch tart

ONE UNBAKED 10-INCH PÂTE BRISÉE TART SHELL (PAGE 198), CHILLED

½ CUP (1 STICK) UNSALTED BUTTER
½ CUP GRANULATED SUGAR
1 EGG
1 CUP FINELY GROUND BLANCHED ALMONDS
3 TABLESPOONS DARK RUM
1 TEASPOON ALMOND EXTRACT
1 TABLESPOON ALL-PURPOSE FLOUR
6 WHITE WINE POACHED PEARS (PAGE 34) IN ½ CUP POACHING LIQUID, COOLED

1. Preheat the oven to 425°.

2. To make the frangipane filling, cream the butter and sugar in the bowl of an electric mixer until light and fluffy. Add the egg, ground almonds, rum, almond extract, and flour, and beat until smooth. Spread the thick mixture evenly in the chilled tart shell and refrigerate it while you prepare the pears.

3. Remove the cooled poached pears from the poaching liquid and cut each in half lengthwise, removing the core and stem. Place each half, cut side down, on a cutting board and cut crosswise into thin slices. Arrange the sliced pear halves on the frangipane around the edge of the tart, leaving space between each half, and place one half in the center of the tart. When arranging the pears, try to "pull" the slices toward the center of the tart, which will elongate the pears a bit and fill the shell better than if the pears were just placed flat. Bake for 45 minutes, or until the tart shell is golden brown and the frangipane has puffed and browned.

4. While the tart is baking, bring the reserved poaching liquid to a boil and reduce by half. Brush this glaze lightly over the fresh-from-the-oven pears. Serve at room temperature.

When I first began entertaining at "lavish" dinner parties, this was one of my favorite desserts. I would poach ripe, firm pears—Bartlett, Comice, or Anjou—in dry white wine or Champagne. The pears were halved, cored, and sliced crosswise, as shown, or lengthwise, and arranged in a pâte brisée or almond crust on a bed of rum-flavored almond filling. As it bakes, the frangipane filling puffs and turns golden around the sliced pears. A 10-inch tart easily serves ten, with a bit left for seconds. Such a tart uses about six pears.

The decorative arrangement of the pears can be varied according to your whim. The pears also can be sliced lengthwise into thin wedges and arranged around the tart as you would do for an apple tart. Pears poached in red wine can be substituted. Glaze the tart with a bit of the poaching liquid, reduced to a thick syrup.

The combination of almonds and pears is a classic one, and this tart belongs in everyone's repertoire.

Pear or Apple Dumplings

These are sweet, homey desserts that can be made with puff pastry or a simple pâte brisée. I have used both types of pastry and been equally satisfied with their flavor and appearance. The puff pastry is a bit lighter, and if you are going to make these several hours before serving, you might find that the puff pastry holds up better. We used Anjou, Bosc, and Red Bartlett pears and good baking-variety apples, such as Cortlands and Ida Reds, and found them all excellent for these individual dumplings.

There are many ways to wrap the fruit. I cut the puff pastry into thick X's and the pâte brisée into equilateral triangles. The pears were gently poached and chilled before they were wrapped. The apples, which tend to bake more quickly than most pears, were not precooked. The stems of the fruit should be left intact if possible, because this makes handling them easier. I like to decorate the encased fruits with pastry leaves and twigs, which I affix with cold water.

(For recipe, see page 40.)

On the pine mantle in our kitchen several plump dumplings await serving. Andy's kerosene lamps and pressed glass candlesticks add a romantic light.

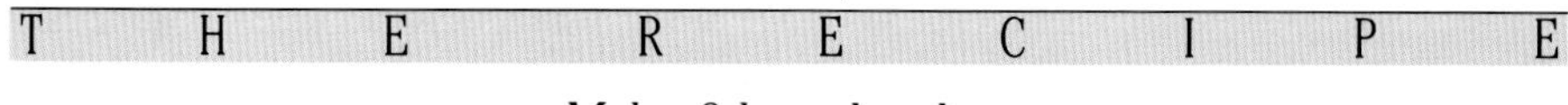

T H E R E C I P E

Makes 8 large dumplings

1 RECIPE PÂTE BRISÉE (PAGE 198) OR 1 POUND PUFF PASTRY (PAGE 206), CHILLED

½ CUP GRANULATED SUGAR
4 TEASPOONS CINNAMON
4 TABLESPOONS (½ STICK) COLD UNSALTED BUTTER, CUT INTO SMALL PIECES
8 POACHED PEARS (PAGE 34), CHILLED AND DRAINED, OR 8 FIRM BUT RIPE APPLES

GLAZE: 1 EGG BEATEN WITH 2 TEASPOONS WATER

1. Roll out the pastry to a thickness of no more than ⅛ inch. Using a sharp paring knife, cut it into 8 rectangles (for puff pastry) or squares (for pâte brisée). Then cut each square into a triangle, or each rectangle into a large X. Cut as many leaf shapes as possible from the pastry scraps, and use the back of the knife to make the vein markings. Keep the pastry chilled on parchment-lined or water-sprayed baking sheets until ready to use.

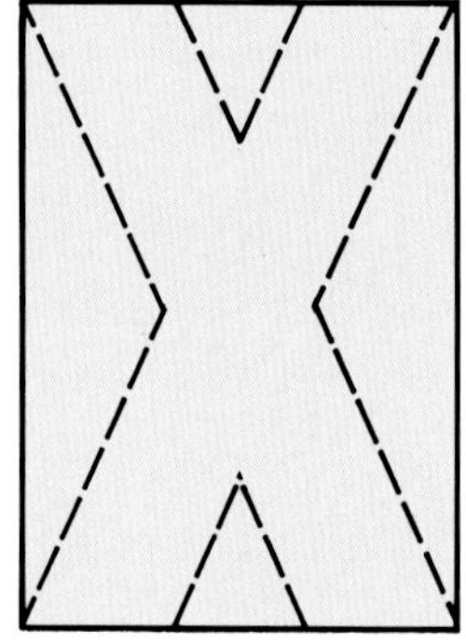

2. Preheat the oven to 400°.

3. Mix the sugar and cinnamon in a small bowl. Set aside. Peel the fruits, but do not remove the stems. Core each piece of fruit carefully from the bottom to within ¾ inch of the top; take care to leave the stem intact. Fill each fruit with some of the sugar-cinnamon mixture and dot with butter. Invert each pear or apple onto the center of a triangle or X of pastry. Bring the edges of the pastry together, moisten them with water, and pinch or press to seal. Garnish the dumplings as desired by pasting the leaves on with water. Place the fruits on a parchment-lined baking sheet and chill until ready to bake.

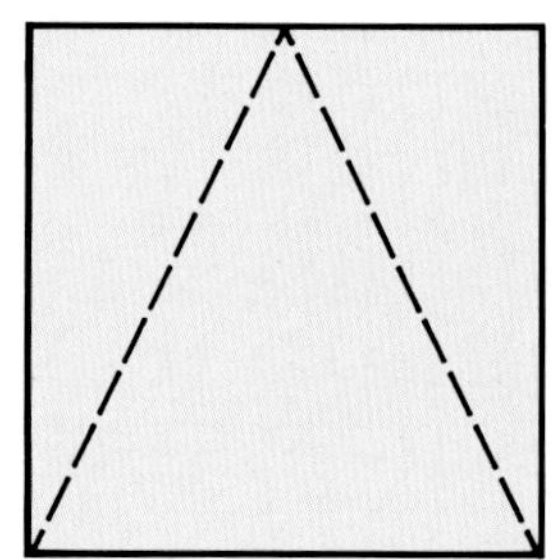

4. Lightly brush each dumpling with egg glaze and bake for approximately 20 to 25 minutes, until the pastry is puffed and nicely browned.

VARIATIONS: The center of each fruit can be filled with dried fruits (Cognac-soaked raisins or currants, chopped dried apricots, etc.) or nuts in addition to the sugar and cinnamon.

Unbaked, pastry-encased apples and pears sit waiting for their egg glaze.

PEARS

Poached Pear Tartlets

Pears poached in Burgundy wine, light, flaky puff pastry, and a bowl of softly whipped heavy cream —alone delightful, together a veritable treat. I prefer using one of the harder pears for poaching—the tall and stately Bosc with its long tapering neck and the plumper green Anjou both have firm flesh with fine texture and flavor. Choose pears that are firm yet ripe, unblemished (any bruises will be magnified by the peeling and poaching), with strong stems.

After I peel the pears very carefully with a swivel-headed potato peeler, being sure to leave the stems intact, I poach them immediately in a barely simmering red wine poaching liquid until they are tender but not soft. I try to refrigerate the poached fruit in the poaching liquid overnight; they take on an even deeper hue and regain some firmness, making the slicing easier.

This is a truly elegant dessert. Wine-poached pears are sliced lengthwise and fanned out over the top of the pastry. The tartlets are served on old Majolica plates on an eighteenth-century "pie crust" table in our parlor.

T H E   R E C I P E

Makes four 4-inch tartlets

¼ POUND PUFF PASTRY (PAGE 206), CHILLED

4 RED WINE POACHED PEARS (PAGE 34)

4 TEASPOONS GRANULATED SUGAR

GLAZE: 1 EGG YOLK BEATEN WITH 1 TEASPOON WATER

GARNISH: SOFTLY WHIPPED CREAM OR DEVON (CLOTTED) CREAM

1. Roll out the pastry to a thickness of ⅛ inch. Using a 4-inch tart ring with a sharp edge or a large biscuit cutter, cut 4 rounds of pastry and place them on a parchment-lined or water-sprayed baking sheet. Chill.

2. Preheat the oven to 400°.

3. Remove the pears from the poaching liquid and drain well. Using a very sharp knife, cut each pear lengthwise into ¼-inch-thick slices to within ¾ inch of the stem. Carefully cut out the slice containing the seeds. Be sure to leave the stem intact. Gently fan out the pear slices and place each pear on a round of puff pastry. Sprinkle each with 1 teaspoon sugar and carefully brush the exposed pastry with the egg glaze. Bake for 20 to 25 minutes, until the pastry is puffed and golden brown. Serve hot or warm with softly whipped cream or a bowl of Devon or clotted cream, available in fine gourmet shops.

NOTE: The puff pastry can be rolled out and cut in advance and refrigerated until you are ready to fill it.

CHAPTER 3.

NOTHING COULD BE BETTER THAN the taste, texture, color, and fragrance of these orchard fruits when picked ripe from the tree. Of course, few of us are lucky enough to have fruit trees in an orchard on our property. But the nurseries have been busy the last two decades developing and propagating a stock of trees that are dwarf or semidwarf in size, meaning that they grow to a height of less than twelve feet at maturity. About ninety percent of the fruits can be picked by someone standing on the ground. These trees are also bred to produce a prodigious number of fruits per branch, earlier than standard-size trees. Such trees are perfect for those of us with limited space but a desire to grow some of our own fruit.

Andy is the orchardman at our house. He plants the trees, prunes them, sprays them, and tells me when the fruits are ready to pick. Pruning is the most difficult and time-consuming part of growing fruit trees, but it is an art when done properly. A perfectly shaped apple tree gives Andy a great sense of accomplishment.

In Westport, there is a store called Hay Day that manages its own orchards and sells produce as close to ripe as possible. All over the country, more and more fruit stands are popping up by the side of the road to offer the small farmer's daily harvest to passersby. This was the norm twenty-five years ago, and I hope it once again becomes a popular way to purchase local produce.

In the following recipes, the fruits are generally interchangeable. The open-faced peach pie can be filled with plums, apricots, or nectarines, and the apricot tarts can be made with small freestone peaches or peeled plums. Galettes—tarts made with a circle of puff pastry—can be topped with any of these fruits, with delicious results.

Peaches, Plums, Apricots & Nectarines

Petal Peach Tart

This unbaked fresh-fruit tart holds four giant Elberta peaches, which are peeled, halved, and sliced. The pieces are arranged in a fully baked petal tart shell. The only cooking the peaches get is the initial poaching in boiling water to loosen the skins, and the slight cooking they might get from the hot apricot–Grand Marnier glaze that is brushed over the fruit.

It is imperative that the peaches chosen for this type of tart be blemishless, firm yet ripe, and large enough so that four peaches, when sliced, will fill the entire tart shell.

The tart shell was made with pâte sucrée, and the reinforced edge was marked with the back of a knife to give it a "barber pole" design. Because there is no extra sugar in this tart, sweetened whipped cream makes a nice topping.

Nasturtiums from August's herb garden decorate this fresh-as-summer peach tart.

THE RECIPE

Makes one 10-inch tart

ONE 10-INCH PETAL-SHAPED PÂTE SUCRÉE TART SHELL (PAGE 202), BAKED AND COOLED

4 GIANT ELBERTA PEACHES

GLAZE: 1 CUP APRICOT PRESERVES
2 TABLESPOONS GRAND MARNIER

1. Peel the peaches by putting them in a large pot of boiling water and removing them with a slotted spoon as soon as the water returns to a boil. When they are cool enough to handle, peel and halve each peach lengthwise and remove the pit. Place each half on a cutting board and cut crosswise into ¼-inch slices, keeping the halves intact. Arrange the cut peach halves in the baked tart shell to resemble a flower, as pictured.

2. Melt the preserves with the Grand Marnier. Strain it and reduce until slightly thickened. Lightly brush the peaches with the glaze and let cool.

Peach Tarte Tatin

A buttery pâte brisée crust lies beneath perfectly arranged quarters of caramelized peaches in this "upside-down" tart.

I used nine large freestone peaches in this tart, which is a variation of the Tarte Tatin on page 9. The skin of the peaches was a lovely deep yellow blushed with pink, so I did not peel the fruit. (The peaches also seem to keep their shape better when left unpeeled.)

Because the fruit is cooked in a golden brown caramel and then reversed onto a platter, the design of the fruit arrangement is very important. Half a peach is centered in the tart, and then quarters of peach are arranged around the perimeter, skin side down. Smaller wedges of peach are used to fill in spaces and to pile on top of the bottom layer, so that the finished tart is thick with fruit.

1 Teaspoon

Belle of Georgia Open-Faced Pie

THE RECIPE

Makes one 10-inch pie

ONE UNBAKED 10-INCH PÂTE BRISÉE PIE SHELL (PAGE 198), WELL CHILLED

24 RIPE BELLE OF GEORGIA PEACHES, UNPEELED, PITTED, AND SLICED
¼ CUP SIFTED ALL-PURPOSE FLOUR
½ TO ¾ CUP GRANULATED SUGAR, OR TO TASTE
2 TABLESPOONS COLD UNSALTED BUTTER, CUT INTO SMALL PIECES
JUICE OF ¼ LEMON

GARNISH: WHIPPED CREAM (OPTIONAL)

1. Preheat the oven to 400°. Fill the pastry with the sliced peaches.

2. Combine the flour and sugar, and sprinkle evenly over the peaches. Dot with butter, and sprinkle on the lemon juice. Bake for approximately 50 minutes, until the pastry is golden brown, the peaches are tender, and the juice from the peaches is bubbling. Let cool slightly before serving with softly whipped cream, if desired.

When Andy and I first found our house on Turkey Hill Road in Westport, Connecticut, more than thirteen years ago, the very first thing we did, even before taking title, was to plant forty-five fruit trees in what was to be our orchard. At that time, we had just an old run-down farmhouse, sorely in need of repair and restoration, and two unplanted acres. The trees were ordered from Henry Leuthardt Nurseries in East Moriches, Long Island, because at that time his catalog had the most intriguing variety of fruits and berries. All of the original trees have survived except the nectarines and five plum trees.

The two white peach trees, Belle of Georgia, thrived, and each year we harvest bushels of peaches, which I use in many ways. These small peaches have excellent flavor and are the most aromatic of all peaches. There are other white varieties—such as Champion and Dwarf Polly—but I like Belle of Georgia the best.

My favorite use for the flavorful Belle-of-Georgia peach is an open-faced pie piled high with fruit, like this one served from an old blue-rimmed breadboard. The blueware bowls are part of a nest I found in an antiques store on the eastern shore of Maryland.

A bottom-crust pie is certainly one of the easiest, homiest pies to make. If you think ahead and have several large rounds of pastry rolled out and frozen between sheets of plastic wrap in your freezer, this type of pie can be put together in minutes and enjoyed with very little fuss. We used firm but ripe dark purple Friar plums, cut into wedges. Apples, apricots, pears, nectarines, and peaches could be substituted and flavorings slightly varied to make equally wonderful pies. (Flavor quarters of cut-up apples with butter, cinnamon, and lemon juice; apricots with just butter and sugar; pears with butter, mace, and sugar; nectarines with butter, sugar, and grated lemon peel; and peaches with butter, sugar, and lime juice.)

Bottom-Crust Plum Pie

THE RECIPE

Makes one 8-inch pie

ONE 14-INCH CIRCLE OF PÂTE BRISÉE (PAGE 198), CHILLED

- **2½ POUNDS FIRM DARK PURPLE PLUMS (FRIAR OR ITALIAN PRUNE PLUMS), WASHED, PITTED, AND QUARTERED**
- **⅓ CUP SIFTED ALL-PURPOSE FLOUR**
- **½ CUP GRANULATED SUGAR**
- **¼ TEASPOON FRESHLY GRATED NUTMEG**
- **JUICE OF ½ LEMON**
- **2 TABLESPOONS COLD UNSALTED BUTTER, CUT INTO SMALL PIECES**
- **MILK OR CREAM (OPTIONAL)**
- **CONFECTIONERS' SUGAR**

1. Preheat the oven to 400°.

2. Put the plum quarters in a large mixing bowl and toss with the flour, sugar, nutmeg, and lemon juice.

3. Place the chilled pastry in an 8-inch pie plate and mound the plums on top. Dot with butter and fold the pastry overhang up over the fruit. Brush the pastry with milk or cream, if desired. Bake for approximately 40 minutes, or until the plums are tender, the juices in the center of the pie are bubbling, and the pastry is golden brown. Let cool slightly before dusting with confectioners' sugar and serving.

This quick and easy plum pie sits amidst a collection of nineteenth-century French painted redware in Pat Guthman's Bee in the Kitchen shop.

There is one very good test for perfectly ripe fruit—and this applies to plums, peaches, nectarines, apricots, pears, pineapples, strawberries, and most melons. The test is fragrance. If a fruit smells ripe and sweet, it is generally ripe. If, in addition, the skin yields to slight pressure of your fingers without feeling too soft, then the fruit is probably ready to eat.

Plums are one of the most difficult fruits to choose. Often they look perfect, plump, and juicy, but are really hard and tasteless. For this reason, I never buy fruits that are prepackaged in plastic.

We had five wonderful plum trees in our first orchard—a very large semidwarf Shropshire Damson, which produced many plums for preserving and tartlets; a Reine Claude, or greengage, which was very juicy and rich in flavor; a German prune, which is reputedly the oldest plum under cultivation, and whose freestone nature made it a delight to use in tarts and kuchens; a Shiro plum, which is small, golden, and perfect for baking; and a Santa Rosa, which produced sweet-sour fruit of great flavor. After thriving for six years, the plum trees all contracted a peculiar disease that no amount of spraying or pruning could control, and all of them had to be pulled up. We're trying again this year.

European Plum Tarts

THE RECIPE

Makes one 7½-inch tart

ONE 7½-INCH PÂTE BRISÉE TART SHELL (PAGE 198), PARTIALLY BAKED AND COOLED

4 TO 5 MEDIUM-SIZE FIRM BUT RIPE PLUMS (FRIAR, AUTUMN ROSA, AND SANTA ROSA ARE GOOD CHOICES)

2 TABLESPOONS UNSALTED BUTTER, AT ROOM TEMPERATURE

Custard

1 EGG

⅓ CUP GRANULATED SUGAR

¼ CUP ALL-PURPOSE FLOUR

¾ CUP HEAVY CREAM

4 TABLESPOONS COGNAC

¼ CUP VANILLA SUGAR (SEE NOTE, PAGE 55)

1. Preheat the oven to 375°.

2. Rub each plum with approximately 1 teaspoon softened butter, and either halve or cut it into eighths. Arrange the plums as desired in the tart shell, and bake for about 15 minutes to soften the fruit.

3. While the tart is baking, prepare the custard. Beat the egg and sugar until thick and pale yellow. Add the flour and mix until smooth. Beat in the cream and Cognac. Spoon the custard around the bottom of the softened plums and sprinkle with vanilla sugar. Return the tart to the oven and bake for approximately 20 minutes, until the custard is puffed and golden. Let cool before serving.

VARIATION: Four 4-inch tartlets can be made by cutting the plums into small wedges and spooning approximately ⅓ cup of custard into each partially baked tartlet shell.

Fragrant plum tarts and tartlets, made with fruits baked European-style in a delicate custard, are set out to cool on my porch steps.

Kelsey Plum Tartlets

A refreshing summer dessert like this is wonderful served poolside on clear glass Depression plates.

These tartlets are very easy last-minute desserts, and so delicious! If you are organized enough to have a plastic container full of baked tartlet shells in the freezer, this dessert will take about twenty minutes to assemble and bake.

I like to use unusual or colorful fruits in this type of simple tartlet. Kelsey plums are becoming increasingly popular—they are good for eating as well as for baking and preserving. If our Reine Claude plum trees are behaving and producing fruits, we will use them. They are more commonly known as "greengage" and are paler green than Kelsey, and possibly even more delicious.

These tartlets could be made with many other fruits, and of course you can use Stanleys, Santa Rosas, or any other large, firm, sweet plum. Generally I peel the plums. If using peaches, I often don't bother. Apricots and pears are left unpeeled, as are nectarines.

You will notice that this recipe, as well as several others in the book, calls for vanilla sugar. I find that the natural flavor and scent of real vanilla beans adds something special to baked fruits, especially in these simple tarts and tartlets. Vanilla sugar is simple to make, and you can maintain a jar for years by adding fresh beans and new sugar, and by keeping the jar sealed airtight.

THE RECIPE

Makes four 4-inch tartlets

FOUR 4-INCH PÂTE BRISÉE TARTLET SHELLS (PAGE 198), PARTIALLY BAKED AND COOLED

- 2 LARGE RIPE KELSEY OR GREENGAGE PLUMS
- 2 TABLESPOONS COLD UNSALTED BUTTER
- 4 TEASPOONS VANILLA SUGAR (SEE NOTE BELOW)
- ½ CUP HEAVY CREAM

GARNISH: FRESH MINT LEAVES

1. Preheat the oven to 375°.

2. Bring a large pot of water to a boil, immerse the plums in the water, and as soon as the water boils again, remove the plums with a slotted spoon. When they are cool enough to handle, remove the skins with a sharp knife, halve the plums lengthwise, and discard the pits. Place one half, cut side down, in each tartlet shell, dot with ½ tablespoon butter, and sprinkle with 1 teaspoon vanilla sugar. Bake for approximately 15 minutes, until the fruit is juicy and tender. Let cool slightly.

3. To serve, pour approximately 2 tablespoons cream carefully around the bottom of each plum half, and garnish with a mint leaf.

NOTE: To make vanilla sugar, store one or more vanilla beans in a tightly closed jar of granulated sugar for a few weeks. Vanilla sugar keeps indefinitely, and you can simply add more sugar to the jar as necessary. Not only does this recipe produce a wonderfully flavored sugar, it is also an excellent way to keep vanilla beans fresh and plump. I purchase vanilla beans in bulk from a spice market and store them this way.

Apricot Tart

We now have over a hundred trees in our orchard, but for some unknown reason, we have had no luck at all growing apricots. But I'm sure we'll try again this year to find two or three trees that will make it at our place.

During the very short commercial apricot season, I scour the markets for firm, fragrant, ripe, perfectly textured fruit. While working on this book, I found excellent apricots from California for three weeks in the latter part of August. I bought them in case lots and made tart after tart, pies, jams, chutneys, and fruit compotes, and ate prodigious numbers of them straight out of the box. There are very few fruits that have all the good qualities of a fine apricot, and an open-faced tart of tender apricot halves, coated with homemade apricot glaze spiked with Grand Marnier, has few equals.

THE RECIPE

Makes one 11-inch tart

ONE 11-INCH PÂTE BRISÉE TART SHELL (PAGE 198), PARTIALLY BAKED AND COOLED

12 FIRM BUT RIPE APRICOTS

¼ CUP VANILLA SUGAR (SEE NOTE, PAGE 55)

GLAZE: ½ CUP APRICOT JAM
2 TABLESPOONS GRAND MARNIER

GARNISH: 2 TABLESPOONS SHELLED, SKINNED NATURAL PISTACHIO HALVES (OPTIONAL)

1. Preheat the oven to 375°.

2. To peel the apricots, bring a large pot of water to a boil. Immerse the apricots in the water, return to a boil, and remove the fruit with a slotted spoon after 30 seconds or so. When cool enough to handle, peel the skin off. Halve the apricots lengthwise and remove the pits.

3. To make the glaze, melt the jam with the Grand Marnier and strain it through a fine sieve.

4. Sprinkle the vanilla sugar in the bottom of the tart shell. Arrange the apricots, cut sides down, in the shell and sprinkle with a bit of additional vanilla sugar. Bake for about 10 minutes, until the sugar melts and the juices begin to run from the fruit. Remove from the oven, brush with the glaze, and arrange the pistachios on top, if desired. Let cool before serving.

An elaborate nineteenth-century drawn-work tablecloth is the background for a fresh apricot tart glistening with apricot glaze. The fork is from my collection of French gateau forks.

Nectarine Galette

This is a luxurious yet simple dessert—a light-as-air round of puff pastry topped with thin wedges of fragrant ripe nectarines. Because the nectarines are quite juicy, a bit of flour mixed with sugar is spread over the round of pastry before the fruit is arranged. This helps thicken the juice without compromising the flavor of the nectarines.

Nectarines are challenging the popularity of peaches for several reasons: They are fuzzless and need no peeling for a galette or pie; many are freestone, which makes slicing them easy; they are generally firm, sweet, and juicy. When buying nectarines, look for fragrant, pink-blushed fruits with no blemishes. Growing your own nectarines requires a spraying schedule similar to that for peaches and a careful pruning program for the trees. Our three-year-old trees are extremely prolific, and it is indeed a treat to pick tree-ripened fruits in August and September.

Nectarines can be substituted in any of the peach and apricot recipes. If the recipe calls for peeled fruit, peel the nectarines with a sharp vegetable peeler rather than blanching them, as you would to remove the skin of peaches or apricots.

T H E R E C I P E

Makes one 9-inch tart

ONE 9-INCH ROUND OF PUFF PASTRY (PAGE 206), WELL CHILLED

- **2 TABLESPOONS ALL-PURPOSE FLOUR**
- **½ CUP GRANULATED SUGAR**
- **4 FIRM BUT RIPE UNPEELED NECTARINES, HALVED, PITTED, AND THINLY SLICED**
- **1 TABLESPOON COLD UNSALTED BUTTER, CUT INTO SMALL PIECES**

GLAZE: 1 EGG YOLK BEATEN WITH 1 TABLESPOON HEAVY CREAM

1. Preheat the oven to 400°.
2. Place the circle of puff pastry on a parchment-lined baking sheet. With the tines of a fork, prick the pastry surface except for a ½-inch rim. Sprinkle the punctured area of the circle *only* with the flour and ¼ cup sugar.
3. Starting just inside the unpunctured edge, arrange the nectarine slices, cut edges toward the center, in concentric circles covering the pastry entirely. Brush the egg yolk glaze on just the exposed rim of puff pastry, sprinkle the remaining sugar on top of the fruit, and dot with butter. Bake for 18 to 20 minutes, until the fruit is tender and the pastry has puffed and turned golden brown. Serve immediately.

VARIATIONS: Apples and peaches can be substituted for the nectarines. Flour does not have to be sprinkled on the pastry for these less-watery fruits.

Three galettes cooling on wire racks. Clockwise from top right: *nectarine, apple, and peach. The dried flowers are from photographer Beth Galton's collection.*

TO THE AMERICAN INDIAN, BERRIES were the "gifts of the gods." That was because hundreds of years ago berries of one sort or another—wild strawberries, huckleberries, currants, blackberries, dewberries, elderberries, red and black raspberries—grew plentifully just about everywhere. Today we most often find wild berries along sandy roads, in arid fields, or near old stone walls. Berries grow best in warm sunlight, but mature bushes will sometimes tolerate a degree of shade.

I have always liked to grow berries. The varieties offered the home grower in catalogs is astonishingly large, and the actual growing time required to achieve real production relatively short. Strawberries bear fruit the first year; raspberries, currants, and blackberries generally give a good crop the second year; blueberry and gooseberry bushes should be covered with berries the third season. Most berries require a small amount of pruning or thinning, very little spraying, and little other maintenance.

On our property, I have planted large numbers of raspberries in fifty-foot rows. The canes are supported by a two-level wire trellis Andy designed and built. The currants, gooseberries, and blueberries require no staking, just plenty of space between the plants and rows so that each bush can be walked around. (This makes trimming and picking easier.) I have planted blackberries away from the other bushes because of their rampant growing habits and thorny canes. The strawberries require thinning each season. The plants a friend gave me produce large juicy berries for three weeks, but they have many runners, which develop into new plants and cause diminution of berry size if left unthinned. Fraises des bois must also be thinned, but I find that once every two or three years is sufficient.

Birds, rabbits, mice, and other creatures often do extensive damage to ripening crops of berries, so remember to cover bushes and berry patches with plastic netting.

Berries

Blackberry Heart

This elegant tart was served on a silver gallery tray garnished with White Wing tea roses, whose centers matched the color of the berries. Glasses of blackberry liqueur accompanied the dessert.

I remember when blackberries could be found only in late July or early August, growing wild. Nowadays they are cultivated in many parts of the world, so that they are available in markets several times a year. The berries we buy are sweet, plump, and have fewer seeds than wild berries. The bushes they grow on are uncharacteristically thorn-free, making picking quick and easy. In 1981 Andy and I planted a row of these thornless bushes (Black Satin and Smoothstem) and we are gratified each summer with a large crop of one-inch-long berries, which I use fresh in tarts, pies, jellies, and jams. I also freeze them for use off-season in cobblers, sauces, and steamed puddings.

I especially like blackberries in tarts because they make a dramatic-looking, elegant dessert. This heart-shaped tart is very easy to make. Crème pâtissière flavored with blackberry liqueur is spread in the bottom of the shell; then blackberries are mounded on top of the cream and glazed. I add another layer of unglazed berries to finish the top, because the glaze tends to disguise the shape of the berries.

THE RECIPE

Makes one 7-inch heart-shaped tart

ONE 7-INCH HEART-SHAPED PÂTE BRISÉE TART SHELL (PAGE 198), BAKED AND COOLED

GLAZE: ¾ CUP RED CURRANT JELLY
2 TABLESPOONS BLACKBERRY LIQUEUR

1 CUP CRÈME PÂTISSIÈRE (BELOW), FLAVORED WITH 1 TABLESPOON BLACKBERRY LIQUEUR

2 PINTS FRESH BLACKBERRIES

GARNISH: WHIPPED CREAM

Crème Pâtissière (Pastry Cream)

Makes about 2½ cups

- 1 CUP MILK
- ½ VANILLA BEAN
- ¼ CUP PLUS 1 TABLESPOON GRANULATED SUGAR
- 3 EGG YOLKS
- 1 TABLESPOON CORNSTARCH
- 1 TABLESPOON FLOUR (PREFERABLY RICE FLOUR FOR LIGHTNESS)
- 1 TEASPOON UNSALTED BUTTER
- 1 CUP HEAVY CREAM (OPTIONAL)

1. Melt the red currant jelly with the liqueur over a low flame. Strain through a fine sieve and let cool slightly.

2. To make the crème pâtissière, scald the milk, vanilla bean, and ¼ cup sugar. In a separate bowl, beat the egg yolks with the remaining 1 tablespoon sugar until thick. Sprinkle in the cornstarch and flour and continue beating until well mixed.

3. Remove the vanilla bean from the milk. Beat half the hot milk into the egg yolk mixture. Combine this with the remaining hot milk and quickly bring to a boil, whisking rapidly to prevent scorching. Remove from the heat and pour into a bowl to cool. Rub the top with the butter to prevent a skin from forming. Cover with plastic wrap and let cool completely.

VARIATION: For a lighter crème pâtissière, beat the heavy cream to soft peaks and fold into the cooled crème using a wooden spoon.

4. To assemble the tart, spoon the crème pâtissière evenly into the tart shell and arrange the blackberries (reserving 10 of the most perfect ones) carefully and neatly on top. Brush lightly with the glaze and top with the reserved berries. Refrigerate until ready to serve. Garnish with softly whipped cream.

Heart-Shaped Raspberry Tart

One day while working on this book, I discovered a very useful and interesting thing. I had intended to make quince jelly by reducing a little sweetened quince syrup, but I let the syrup cool before it reached the jelly stage. The syrup reduction was such a lovely pinkish golden color and tasted so good that I used it to sweeten the whipped cream with which I was going to fill the tart shell. The cream thickened up nicely and stayed that way for several hours. (Whipped cream can become watery if not used immediately, but the natural pectin in the quince syrup kept this cream thick.) The flavor was unusual and delicious. I used the same syrup to glaze the red raspberries. Crystal-clear, it was light enough not to obscure the delicacy of the berries in any way.

My favorite heart-shaped tart shell is a perfect base for luscious red raspberries set atop a layer of quince-flavored cream and glazed.

T H E R E C I P E

Makes one 8½-inch heart-shaped tart

ONE 8½-INCH HEART-SHAPED PÂTE BRISÉE TART SHELL (PAGE 198), BAKED AND COOLED

1 PINT HEAVY CREAM
⅓ CUP QUINCE SYRUP (PAGE 211)
3 PINTS FRESH RED RASPBERRIES

GLAZE: ¼ CUP QUINCE JELLY (PAGE 211), MELTED AND COOLED SLIGHTLY

Whip the cream until soft peaks form. Add the quince syrup and whip until stiff. Spread the whipped cream evenly in the tart shell. Carefully arrange half the raspberries on top of the cream, and use the remaining berries to make a neat second layer. Lightly glaze the berries with the melted quince jelly. Serve immediately.

This is a wonderfully easy dessert to make. With some tender baked tartlet shells in the freezer, it's a simple matter to fill them at the last minute with flavored whipped cream and fresh ripe red raspberries.

The variations of this recipe, if you can call this easy but delicious concoction a recipe, are endless. I've made tartlets like this with toppings of sliced gooseberries glazed with apricot jam, wild strawberries sprinkled with sugar, dewberries brushed with dewberry jelly, and black or purple raspberries coated with a thin glaze of red raspberry jelly. This is a fine and tasty way to serve the most perfect berries of the late summer season.

A simple filling of flavored whipped cream is carefully topped with the most perfect berries available. Each tartlet shell is brushed with a bit of red currant glaze before filling so that the crust remains flaky and tender. More glaze is used on top for shine.

Red Raspberry Tartlets

THE RECIPE

Makes four 4-inch tartlets

FOUR 4-INCH PÂTE BRISÉE TARTLET SHELLS (PAGE 198), BAKED AND COOLED

GLAZE: ½ CUP RED CURRANT JELLY

1½ CUPS HEAVY CREAM
1 TABLESPOON FRAMBOISE (OPTIONAL)
1 PINT FRESH RED RASPBERRIES

1. Melt the jelly in a small saucepan and strain. Brush the inside bottom and edges of the baked tartlet shells with a small amount.

2. Whip the cream (with framboise, if desired) to soft peaks and divide evenly among the tartlet shells. Carefully arrange the raspberries on top. Brush with the remaining glaze and chill until ready to serve.

Golden Raspberry Tartlets

Three years ago Andy and I planted a relatively new variety of pale golden-pink everbearing raspberry called Fall Gold. These raspberries are the result of crosses between the red Taylor raspberry, the Fall Red raspberry, and a Korean wild berry. We were rewarded the first fall with unusually large, flavorful, sweet berries, and the next season there were even more.

These unusual, delicious berries create a sensation whenever I use them, in tarts, on wedding cakes, or just by themselves with thick cream. "What's wrong with the red raspberries?" some say, but nevertheless, I am a convert to these beautiful, exotic berries.

These simple tartlets would also be great topped with black raspberries (Allen and Black Hawk are wonderful), or purple raspberries (Royalty). A large rectangular puff pastry tart shell can substitute for the pâte brisée tartlet shells, with spectacular results (see photograph on the following page).

No glaze was used, because the berries are so delicate in flavor and color, but you could use a clear golden raspberry jelly (made from overripe or undersize berries) or quince, sour cherry, or crab apple jelly over the berries.

T H E R E C I P E

Makes four 4-inch tartlets

FOUR 4-INCH PÂTE BRISÉE TARTLET SHELLS (PAGE 198), BAKED AND COOLED

1 CUP CRÈME PÂTISSIÈRE (PAGE 63)

2 PINTS FRESH GOLDEN RASPBERRIES

GLAZE (OPTIONAL): GOLDEN RASPBERRY, QUINCE, SOUR CHERRY, OR CRAB APPLE JELLY (PAGE 211), MELTED WITH 1 TABLESPOON FRAMBOISE, GRAND MARNIER, OR COGNAC

Spoon ¼ cup crème pâtissière evenly into each tartlet shell and arrange the raspberries neatly on top. Glaze very lightly with melted jelly, if desired.

VARIATION: Substitute the seeds of 1 pomegranate for the raspberries, or use a combination of both. When choosing a pomegranate, look for a dark red fruit that is hard and heavy. Score the skin into quarters with the point of a stainless steel knife (don't use carbon steel—it discolors the fruit). With the point of the knife, pry the pomegranate open. Do not cut the fruit or the seeds will be damaged. To dislodge the seeds, use your fingers to break them away from the membrane. Often a fruit that is red on the outside will be pale or even whitish inside. These seeds generally have little or no flavor and must be discarded.

VARIATION: To make Golden Raspberries Milles Feuilles (page 70), substitute a 5 × 19-inch rectangle of puff pastry (page 206) for the tartlet shells.

This four-inch tartlet, served on an amber-pink Depression glass plate and accompanied by a Sauternes, makes a very elegant dessert.

Golden Raspberry Milles Feuilles

A golden raspberry milles feuilles (see Variation, page 68).

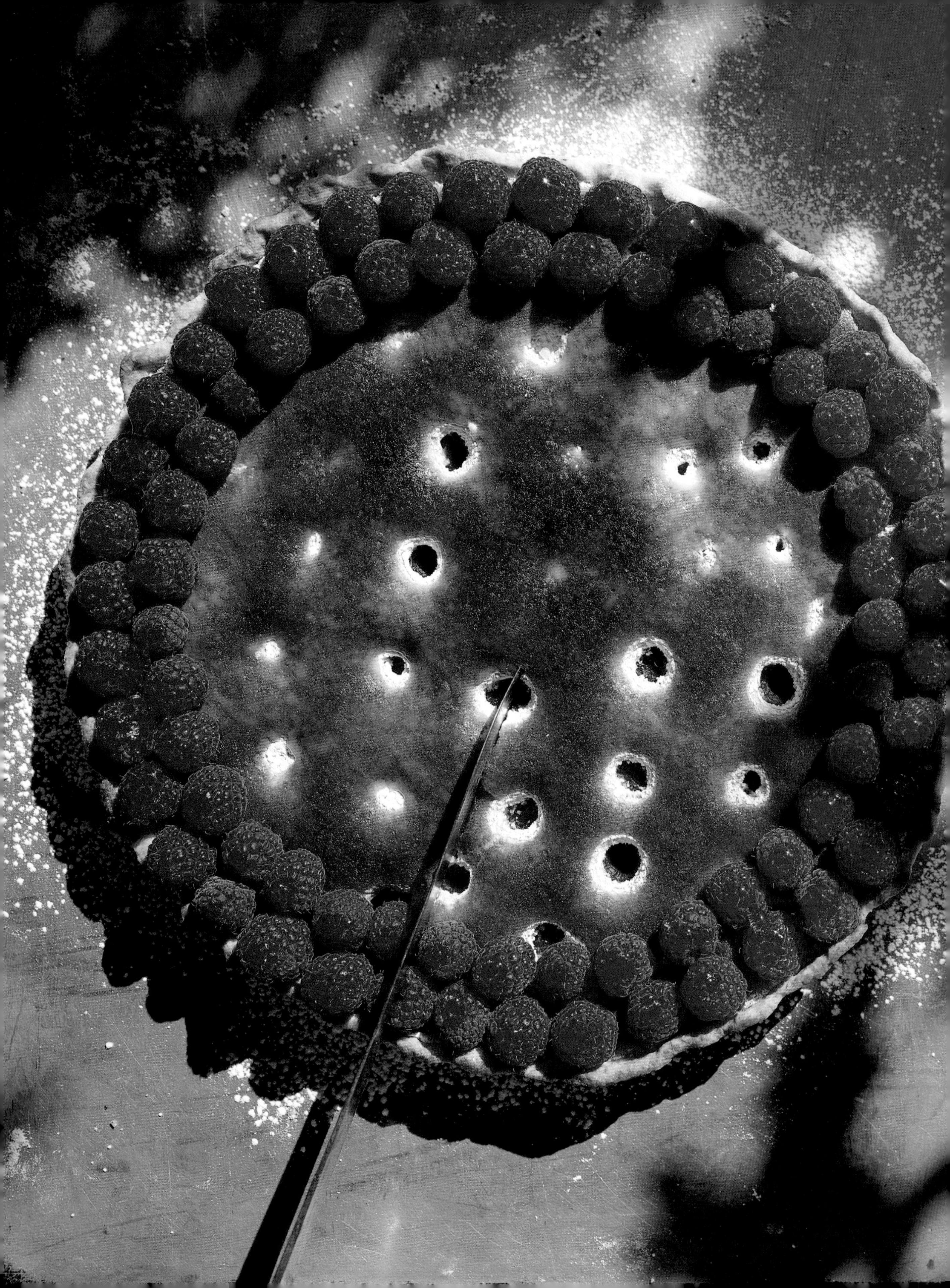

Raspberry Génoise Tart

Last summer, during a trip to Paris to visit Alexis, I went from pâtisserie to pâtisserie sampling all the interesting-looking tarts and tartlets. Several of the most renowned pastry shops were closed for *vacances,* but I discovered a gem of a place on the Left Bank that is, I think, the best in Paris for extremely delicious tarts. It was here at M. Lerch's shop that I ate a version of this raspberry tart, which is baked in a light, buttery génoise batter and glazed with red raspberry jelly.

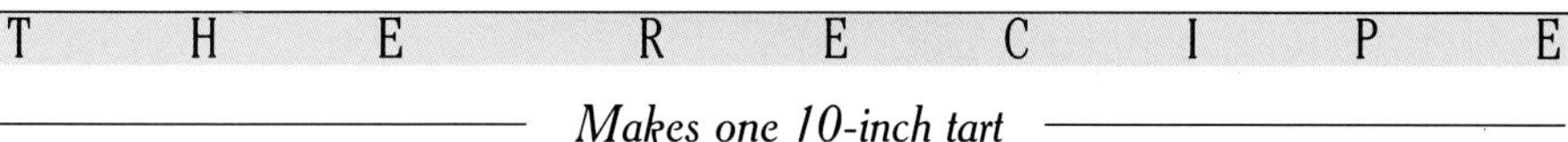

Makes one 10-inch tart

ONE 10-INCH PÂTE BRISÉE TART SHELL (PAGE 198), PARTIALLY BAKED AND COOLED

Génoise

- 3 EGGS
- ½ CUP GRANULATED SUGAR
- ½ TEASPOON VANILLA EXTRACT
- 1 TABLESPOON FRAMBOISE OR GRAND MARNIER
- PINCH OF SALT
- ⅔ CUP SIFTED ALL-PURPOSE FLOUR
- 4 TABLESPOONS (½ STICK) UNSALTED BUTTER, MELTED AND COOLED

- 2 PINTS FRESH RED RASPBERRIES
- CONFECTIONERS' SUGAR

GLAZE: ½ CUP RED RASPBERRY JELLY, MELTED AND STRAINED

1. To make the génoise batter, beat the eggs, sugar, vanilla, framboise, and salt in the bowl of an electric mixer for approximately 10 minutes, until very thick and pale yellow. Quickly but gently fold in a third of the flour. When it is nearly incorporated, fold in a third of the melted butter. Continue folding in the flour and butter alternately until all is incorporated. Do not overmix; the batter should retain its volume.

2. Quickly pour the batter into the partially baked tart shell and arrange about one-fourth of the raspberries (½ pint) on top. Sprinkle with a bit of confectioners' sugar and bake for 15 to 18 minutes, or until the tart shell is golden brown and the génoise springs back when lightly touched. Remove to a rack and let cool.

3. Carefully arrange the remaining raspberries in two rows around the outer edge of the tart, and dot the tops of the berries with the glaze. Serve immediately.

My version of this Parisian specialty was made with home-grown Taylor raspberries and lightly dusted with confectioners' sugar.

Red Currant Tart

We have always had currant bushes. My father grew a couple of bushes in Nutley so that my family could make red currant jelly each year. On our property in Middlefield, Andy and I planted six bushes as soon as we could dig our first garden. Those bushes, uprooted along with our first blueberry bushes and transported to Westport, now grow large and strong in our berry patch and provide us with more than enough currants for jellies, syrups, tarts, and pies.

The variety of currant most commonly offered by catalogs is Red Lake—the largest, sweetest, and finest of all. Currants ripen in late July and early August, are easy to pick, and are very simple to work with. Tarts made with these transparent round berries always look spectacular, and taste even better. When I am using a pâte brisée crust, I mound the berries atop a layer of pastry cream. If I am making a nut crust tart, I simply put the currants in the crust and glaze them with plenty of red currant jelly.

THE RECIPE

Makes one 4¼ × 13¾-inch rectangular tart or one 8-inch heart-shaped tart

1 RECTANGULAR OR HEART-SHAPED PÂTE BRISÉE TART SHELL (PAGE 198), BAKED AND COOLED

1½ CUPS CRÈME PÂTISSIÈRE (PAGE 63)

1½ TO 2 PINTS FRESH RED CURRANTS, CAREFULLY STEMMED

1 CUP RED CURRANT GLAZE (PAGE 211)

Spread the crème pâtissière evenly in the tart shell. Neatly mound the currants on top. Brush or spoon the glaze on the currants. Refrigerate the tart until ready to serve, for at least 1 hour but no longer than 3 hours, or the glaze will become watery and unsightly.

VARIATION: Omitting the crème pâtissière, arrange the berries in a nut crust (page 205) and spoon on the red currant glaze. Refrigerate for 1 to 3 hours. Serve with softly whipped cream, if desired.

The jewel-like red currant tart (left and below) *and strawberry Christmas tree tart* (below and page 76) *made impressive additions to the dessert table at our Christmas party last year. Red currants from New Zealand are generally available in December.*

Strawberry Christmas Tart

Glistening strawberries, halved and glazed, fill this festive tree-shaped tart shell garnished with spruce and holly.

At Christmas Andy and I usually have an "all over the house" late-afternoon party. This year we invited one hundred and fifty friends for a five o'clock dinner buffet. Hors d'oeuvres were served in the house, along with wine, champagne, and eggnog. At six-thirty, guests were invited to go out the back door to my large studio kitchen, where we had arranged two very large buffets of roasted meats, birds, salads, breads, and condiments. After dinner everyone went once again into the main house for desserts set out in the dining room—a croquembouche, a bûche de Noël seven feet long, fruitcakes, plum puddings, freshly stewed fruits, berry tarts, and a gingerbread mansion aglow with light (see photograph on the preceding page).

To make the strawberry Christmas tart for the dessert display, I used a wonderful tree-shaped Mexican tin cake pan someone gave me long ago. I lined it with pâte brisée and used it just as I would a regular tart shell. It worked very well and added a festive touch to the table.

T H E R E C I P E

Makes 1 large tart (our Christmas tree pan measures 12 inches long and 9 inches at the base)

1 LARGE PÂTE BRISÉE TART SHELL (PAGE 198), BAKED AND COOLED

2 CUPS CRÈME PÂTISSIÈRE (PAGE 63) OR STIFFLY WHIPPED CREAM

4 PINTS LARGE FRESH STRAWBERRIES, HULLED AND HALVED LENGTHWISE

½ TO ¾ CUP RED CURRANT GLAZE (PAGE 211)

Spread the crème pâtissière evenly in the bottom of the tart shell. Neatly arrange the berries over the cream in overlapping rows so that they do not lie flat on the cream but incline slightly upright. Lightly brush or spoon the glaze over the berries. Refrigerate until ready to serve, for 1 to 3 hours.

NOTE: The large berries must be halved. If they are not pointy, but instead broadly shaped at the tip, halve them lengthwise through the narrowest part so they look more pointed.

Sliced Strawberry Heart

This heart-shaped tart is a variation of the Strawberry Christmas Tart (opposite). The shell was fashioned from puff pastry instead of pâte brisée, and the strawberries were sliced lengthwise. No pastry cream was used, as the tart was served with a bowl of softly whipped sweetened cream.

Cut-glass cake stands on lace doilies hold two hearts made from puff pastry and filled with sliced strawberries glazed with melted quince jelly.

THE RECIPE

Makes one 7- to 8½-inch tart

ONE HEART-SHAPED PUFF PASTRY TART SHELL (PAGE 206), BAKED AND COOLED

2 TO 3 PINTS FRESH STRAWBERRIES, HULLED AND SLICED LENGTHWISE

GLAZE: ½ CUP QUINCE JELLY (PAGE 211), MELTED AND COOLED

GARNISH: WHIPPED CREAM SWEETENED WITH QUINCE SYRUP (PAGE 211)

Arrange the strawberry slices, pointed ends up, as desired in the tart shell. Lightly spoon the glaze on top of the berries, covering them well, and chill. Serve with quince-flavored whipped cream.

Fraises des Bois Tartlets

Fraises des bois are fragrant woodland strawberries of European origin, favored by herb- and perennial-border gardeners. The plants are compact and bushy, producing a succession of berries throughout the summer. There are only two requirements for growing your own fraises: plant an excellent variety—White Flower Farms recommends Charles V—and continually pick the ripening berries. My fraises patch began with a gift of ten plants in 1973. With a thinning and dividing program every two years, our garden now boasts hundreds of healthy, productive plants, which line the edges of paths and border the brick-enclosed flower beds. Although these berries can tolerate a degree of shade, I get larger, sweeter berries when the plants are set in full sun.

These are rather large, deep tartlets. I like them large to make the most of the great beauty of the fraises des bois. So as not to detract in any way from the unique taste of the berries, the filling of either sweetened whipped cream or crème fraîche is deliberately plain. Crème pâtissière or a vanilla Bavarian cream filling could be used as an alternative, however.

T H E   R E C I P E

Makes two deep 5-inch tartlets

TWO DEEP 5-INCH PÂTE BRISÉE TARTLET SHELLS (PAGE 198), BAKED AND COOLED

1 CUP HEAVY CREAM OR CRÈME FRAÎCHE

1 PINT FRAISES DES BOIS

1 TABLESPOON GRANULATED SUGAR *OR* 1 TEASPOON VANILLA EXTRACT (OPTIONAL)

1. Whip the cream or crème fraîche to soft peaks, adding sugar or vanilla extract, if desired, after the cream begins to thicken. Chill.

2. To assemble the tart, spoon the whipped cream into the tartlet shells and arrange the fraises des bois on top, stem ends down. Garnish with a small stem of berries. Serve immediately.

VARIATION: Substitute crème pâtissière (page 63) or a vanilla Bavarian cream filling for the whipped cream.

A sprig of tiny fraises des bois decorates the top of this deep, cream-filled tartlet for two. An antique cut-glass saucer of champagne flavored with strawberry liqueur was a fitting accompaniment for this Baroque musicale.

I like to make blueberry tarts when our blueberries are being harvested, so that I can use the largest and most luscious berries.

Of all the garden varieties of berries, blueberries are the slowest to bear fruit, but by far the most long lived once they are established. We planted a range of berry bushes so that our harvest would be long. Last year we picked berries from early August through the end of October, although such a long picking season is unusual. We bought our original bushes from Leuthardt in Long Island and have several Earliblues, Collins, Jerseys, and Covilles. Four years ago we planted some Atlantics, and this year we plan to establish another row of New Herberts—whose berries are reported to be an inch in diameter. When planting blueberry bushes, be sure to plant at least two different varieties, for pollination and heaviest fruit production.

We use the berries in tarts, pies, and muffins. Andy loves my blueberry crumb cake, too. I freeze quantities of berries on baking sheets and pack them in rigid containers for winter use. When they are frozen this way, little of the flavor is lost, and the berries tend to be less watery than if frozen with sugar or syrup.

Blueberry Tart

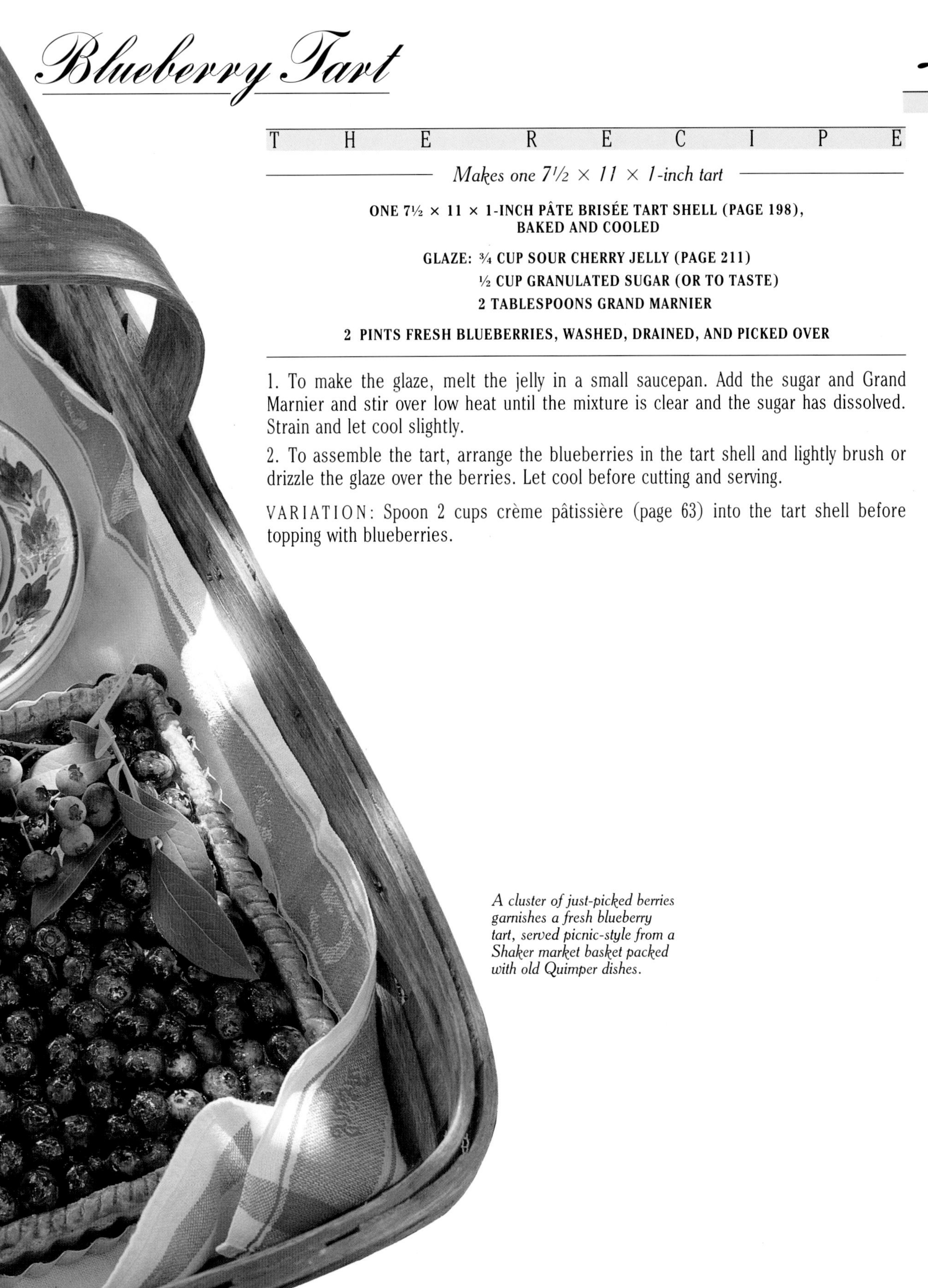

T H E R E C I P E

Makes one 7½ × 11 × 1-inch tart

ONE 7½ × 11 × 1-INCH PÂTE BRISÉE TART SHELL (PAGE 198), BAKED AND COOLED

GLAZE: ¾ CUP SOUR CHERRY JELLY (PAGE 211)
½ CUP GRANULATED SUGAR (OR TO TASTE)
2 TABLESPOONS GRAND MARNIER

2 PINTS FRESH BLUEBERRIES, WASHED, DRAINED, AND PICKED OVER

1. To make the glaze, melt the jelly in a small saucepan. Add the sugar and Grand Marnier and stir over low heat until the mixture is clear and the sugar has dissolved. Strain and let cool slightly.

2. To assemble the tart, arrange the blueberries in the tart shell and lightly brush or drizzle the glaze over the berries. Let cool before cutting and serving.

VARIATION: Spoon 2 cups crème pâtissière (page 63) into the tart shell before topping with blueberries.

A cluster of just-picked berries garnishes a fresh blueberry tart, served picnic-style from a Shaker market basket packed with old Quimper dishes.

Blueberry Pie

This is one of those oddities that was bound to appear in a book about pies and tarts—a deep pie baked in a tart shell with a decorative top crust.

Fresh blueberries are so good, with such a unique flavor, that I hesitate to put anything in either a pie or a tart that would detract from that flavor. Thus, my blueberry pie contains nothing but blueberries, some sugar, flour for thickening the juices, and a bit of butter to enhance the berry flavor. I don't like spices like nutmeg or cardamom with blueberries, and I find even lemon juice superfluous.

Fresh blueberries are by far the best for pies—either the large cultivated blueberries or the tiny, less sweet "huckleberries" from the mountainous regions in the northern sections of the United States. Frozen berries can be used, but often they make a watery pie lacking depth of flavor.

This pie has a very decorative top crust. Leaves, in this case blueberry-type leaves, are cut from a circle of pastry and arranged over the top of the pie. Then the crust is glazed with an egg yolk and cream mixture and sprinkled with sugar, which makes it glisten.

A blueberry pie, fresh from the oven and topped with a "crust" of pastry leaves, cools on an antique wire rack. Tartlet shells—made from pastry scraps—and jars of homemade red currant and sour cherry jelly rest on the windowsill.

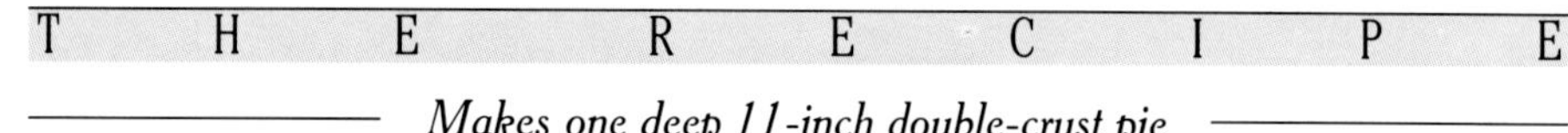

THE RECIPE

Makes one deep 11-inch double-crust pie

PÂTE BRISÉE (PAGE 198) FOR AN 11-INCH DOUBLE-CRUST PIE, CHILLED

3 PINTS FRESH BLUEBERRIES, WASHED, DRAINED, AND PICKED OVER

⅓ TO ½ CUP SIFTED ALL-PURPOSE FLOUR

1 CUP PLUS 1 TABLESPOON GRANULATED SUGAR

1 TABLESPOON UNSALTED BUTTER, CUT INTO SMALL PIECES

GLAZE: 1 EGG BEATEN WITH ½ CUP HEAVY CREAM

1. Preheat the oven to 400°. Roll out half the pastry dough into a circle large enough to fit a 2-inch-deep 11-inch tart pan. Line the pan and refrigerate.

2. Roll out the remaining pastry to a thickness of ⅛-inch and cut out leaf shapes using a sharp paring knife. Make the veins of the leaves by pressing the back of the knife into the leaf. Transfer to a parchment-lined or water-sprayed baking sheet, cover, and refrigerate until ready to use.

3. Put the blueberries in a large mixing bowl and sprinkle with the flour, 1 cup sugar, and the butter. Gently toss so that the berries are completely covered.

4. Brush the entire pastry crust (edges and bottom) with the egg glaze and pour the blueberries into the shell. Decoratively arrange the leaves on top of the fruit, covering it almost completely. Brush the leaves with the egg glaze and sprinkle with 1 tablespoon sugar. Bake the pie for 50 minutes, or until the blueberry juices have bubbled and thickened. Let cool completely on a wire rack before cutting.

Traditionally cranberries are used in dressings or relishes accompanying Thanksgiving or Christmas turkey. Several years ago I began making desserts out of cranberries, and the cranberry tart in a crust of pâte brisée or a nut crust became one of my family's favorites.

This is a very easy tart to make—the fresh cranberries are cooked with sugar, red currant jelly, and Cognac until tender but not popped. Softened gelatin is added to thicken the filling before it is poured into the tart shell and chilled.

A large cranberry tart awaits our holiday dinner guests. The glass turkeys and pressed glass goblets (here filled with liqueur-spiked cranberry juice) are early twentieth-century in origin.

Cranberry Tart

THE RECIPE

Makes one 10-inch tart

ONE 10-INCH PÂTE BRISÉE TART SHELL (PAGE 198) OR ALMOND NUT CRUST (PAGE 205), BAKED AND COOLED

- **2 ENVELOPES UNFLAVORED GELATIN**
- **½ CUP COLD WATER**
- **6 CUPS (3 12-OUNCE PACKAGES) FRESH CRANBERRIES**
- **1¾ TO 2 CUPS SUGAR, TO TASTE**
- **1 CUP RED CURRANT JELLY**
- **2 TABLESPOONS COGNAC**

1. Soften the gelatin in the cold water.

2. To make the filling, combine the cranberries, sugar, jelly, and Cognac in a saucepan and cook over low heat for 10 minutes. Do not overcook or the mixture will become too watery; the cranberries should be soft but not bursting. Remove from the heat and let cool slightly. Stir in the gelatin and let cool completely.

3. Pour the cranberry filling into the tart shell of your choice and chill for at least 1 hour.

CHAPTER 5.

UNTIL ANDY BUILDS ME AN ORANGERY I will have to be content to buy citrus fruit at my local markets. I envy my lucky friends in the South and in California, who are able to go outdoors and pick a lemon for tea, a grapefruit for breakfast, or oranges for juice. On a recent trip to Los Angeles, I stopped by my friend Joan Baeder's house on the way to the airport. She rushed outside, picked an armful of lemons, and squeezed them for a large pitcher of fresh lemonade. It was such a simple gesture, but I was touched by the thoughtfulness of it.

Lemons, limes, oranges, and other citrus fruits—like Key limes and clementines—make wonderful pies and tarts. Clementines and Key limes are local fruits and are available only a short time each year. But large seedless lemons, Persian limes, and most oranges can be found year-round at markets. Many of the recipes in this chapter use not only the juice from these fruits but also the grated rind, the zest, candied strips of the peel, or whole, thin slices of the fruit and rind, cooked and candied.

I prefer my lemon tarts tart and my Key lime pies not too sweet, so I have reduced the traditional amounts of sugar by approximately one-third. If you have a sweeter tooth than I do, you could add a bit more sugar to the recipes in this chapter.

Citrus Fruits

Shaker Lemon Pie

Lemon pie cooling on the Shaker cupboard in our new kitchen. Andy's old yellow-ware bowls are filled with the simple ingredients—eggs, sugar, and lemons.

Our Massachusetts cottage is quite near the Hancock Shaker Village. Each year, to celebrate the restoration of the village, there is a three-day festival. I first tasted a slice of lemon pie at Hancock, and loved its sour-sweet taste and flaky crust.

The lemons *must* be sliced paper-thin if this pie is to be edible. Otherwise, the lemons and the peels will be too tough to eat; no amount of baking will tenderize them. This recipe makes an 11-inch pie; half the recipe is enough filling for an 8-inch pie.

The crust turns a rich golden brown color if an egg white glaze is brushed on before baking. To accentuate the fact that it is a lemon-slice pie, I cut long slices into the top crust so that the bright yellow filling shows through.

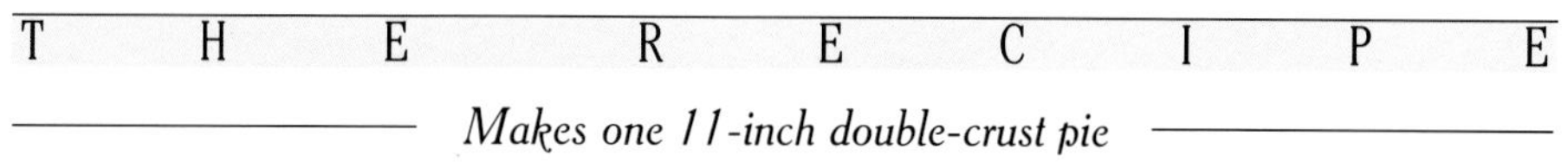

Makes one 11-inch double-crust pie

TWO 11-INCH CIRCLES OF PÂTE BRISÉE (PAGE 198), CHILLED

4 LARGE LEMONS
4 CUPS GRANULATED SUGAR
9 EGGS, WELL BEATEN

GLAZE: 2 EGG WHITES, BEATEN WITH A FORK

1. Wash and cut 2 of the lemons into paper-thin slices. (It is very important to slice the lemons as thinly as possible; use a very sharp knife or an electric meat slicer, if one is available.) Remove the peel and pith of the 2 remaining lemons; slice the flesh very, very thinly, and put it with the other slices in a large mixing bowl. Add the sugar and toss well to coat all the lemon slices. Cover the bowl with plastic wrap and let the mixture rest overnight, stirring occasionally. This takes the bitterness from the rind.

2. The next day, preheat the oven to 450°. Press one circle of pastry into an 11-inch pie plate and chill.

3. Add the beaten eggs to the sugar-coated lemon slices and mix well. Turn the mixture into the prepared pie shell, neatly arranging some of the lemon slices on top. Cut long, even slashes 1 inch apart in the other pastry round and cover the filling with it. Crimp the edges of the pie to seal. Brush the pastry top and edges with the egg white glaze. Bake for 15 minutes. Reduce the oven temperature to 375° and continue baking for 30 minutes, or until the crust is golden brown and shiny. Let cool on a rack before serving.

Donna Scott's Tarte au Citron

Donna worked as a chef in our catering business for a year, and she often baked this tarte au citron. Made in a deep pie shell, the tart is served at room temperature and is dusted with confectioners' sugar right before being sliced.

I love lemon tarts. When I enter a new pastry shop or look at the dessert menu of a restaurant, I invariably order whatever is lemon. I can recall every great tart I have tasted—the tarte au citron at Fauchon in Paris, the lemon tart at the Hotel Meridien's Maurice Restaurant in New York, and the lemon soufflé tart at Hubert's in New York are just three of many that linger in my memory. Donna's tart is delicious, a combination of sour lemon and ground almonds in a thick custard. The crust is a buttery pâte brisée.

T H E R E C I P E

Makes two 8-inch tarts or one deep 9-inch pie

TWO UNBAKED 8-INCH PÂTE BRISÉE TART SHELLS OR ONE DEEP UNBAKED 9-INCH PÂTE BRISÉE PIE SHELL (PAGE 198), CHILLED

- **6 EGGS**
- **1 CUP GRANULATED SUGAR**
- **JUICE AND GRATED RIND OF 4 LEMONS**
- **1½ CUPS (3 STICKS) UNSALTED BUTTER, MELTED AND COOLED**
- **1 CUP SLIVERED OR SLICED BLANCHED ALMONDS**
- **½ TEASPOON ALMOND EXTRACT**
- **1 TEASPOON VANILLA EXTRACT**
- **CONFECTIONERS' SUGAR**

1. Preheat the oven to 375°.

2. Combine the eggs and 1 cup minus 2 tablespoons sugar in a bowl and whisk by hand until the mixture is pale and thick and forms a ribbon. Add the lemon juice and rind and the butter and stir until thoroughly combined.

3. Put the almonds, almond extract, and reserved 2 tablespoons sugar in the bowl of a food processor, and process until the almonds are very finely ground. Stir the almonds into the egg-sugar mixture and add the vanilla. Pour the mixture into the chilled pastry shells and bake for 30 minutes, or until the tops of the tarts begin to brown. Lower the oven temperature to 350° and bake for approximately 25 minutes more, until the filling is set. Remove the tarts to a rack to cool before dusting with confectioners' sugar and serving.

NOTE: This tart is delicious served with softly whipped cream, sweetened with a very small amount of granulated sugar and a few drops of almond extract, if desired.

The tart—nicely browned and dusted with confectioners' sugar—is served on colorful turquoise and yellow Fiestaware.

I love lemon tarts of any kind so long as they taste of fresh, tart lemons, are not too sweet, and are beautiful. This dessert was named a damask tart because the decoration of the candied lemon peel atop the tart was applied in a damask pattern. The crust is made in the shape of a deep heart—one of a series of heart rings I purchased in Paris, which are obtainable in some stores here. The filling is a sour lemon mousse—very light, fluffy, and creamy. There are no egg yolks in this mousse, which accounts for its almost white color. The tart must be made several hours before serving—the mousse takes that long to set—so that it can be easily cut.

Lemon Mousse Damask Tart

T H E R E C I P E

Makes one 7-inch heart-shaped tart

ONE 7-INCH HEART-SHAPED PÂTE BRISÉE TART SHELL (PAGE 198), BAKED AND COOLED

1 ENVELOPE UNFLAVORED GELATIN
1 TABLESPOON COLD WATER
½ CUP FRESHLY SQUEEZED LEMON JUICE
1 CUP GRANULATED SUGAR
7 EGG WHITES
1 CUP HEAVY CREAM
GRATED RIND OF 1 LEMON

GARNISH: CANDIED LEMON PEEL (PAGE 101)

1. In a small heavy saucepan, soften the gelatin in the water. Add the lemon juice and sugar and stir over a very low flame just until the gelatin is thoroughly dissolved. Do not let it boil or cook too long. Remove from the heat and let cool to a syruplike consistency over a bowl of ice water. This mixture must be completely cooled before being added to the egg whites.

2. Beat the egg whites until very stiff. Still mixing, slowly add the gelatin mixture. Whip the cream until stiff and gently fold it in. Take care to thoroughly incorporate all ingredients without deflating the egg whites and cream. Finally, fold in the grated rind.

3. Mound the mousse in the baked tart shell and chill for at least 4 hours. Garnish with candied lemon peel and serve.

This lemon tart, decorated with candied lemon peel, is served from a copper heart-shaped tray lined with shiny lemon leaves. It rests on a silk damask background.

Lemon Curd Tarts

Lemon curd, with its five basic ingredients (I include both the lemon juice and the grated rind), should be one of the simpler fillings to make. Nevertheless, the method of cooking and the proportions of the ingredients required vary radically from recipe to recipe. The final product is often too sweet, too thin, too sour, or tasteless.

This recipe has been my favorite for many years. I make several batches of it at one time (I never double the recipe because it takes much longer to thicken; I always make it just as I have written it) and keep it refrigerated in glass jars for up to three weeks. It is a wonderful filling for tarts and tartlets, a great spread on toast, and can be lightened for a mousselike dessert with folded-in whipped cream.

When I made the curd for the photograph, I made it in two batches. One batch was made with my own homegrown eggs and the other with store-bought eggs. My eggs produced a curd that was far superior in color, texture, and thickness. I always try to use my own eggs in baking and cooking, and after this unplanned experiment, I will continue to do so. If you can't raise your own hens, do shop for very fresh eggs, or farm-raised eggs.

Two lemon tarts ready to be served on a tea table on our upper porch, which looks out over Long Island Sound. The plates and tea cups are English lustre.

The deeper yellow lemon curd tart was made with eggs from my own hens.

T H E R E C I P E

Makes one 7½-inch tart or four 4-inch tartlets

ONE 7½-INCH PÂTE BRISÉE TART SHELL (PAGE 198) OR FOUR 4-INCH PÂTE SUCRÉE TARTLET SHELLS (PAGE 202), BAKED AND COOLED

6 EGG YOLKS, BEATEN
1 CUP GRANULATED SUGAR
½ CUP FRESHLY SQUEEZED LEMON JUICE
½ CUP (1 STICK) UNSALTED BUTTER, CUT INTO SMALL PIECES
1 TABLESPOON GRATED LEMON RIND

1. To make the lemon curd, strain the beaten egg yolks through a sieve into a medium-size heavy saucepan. Add the sugar and lemon juice, stir to combine, and cook over low heat, stirring constantly, for about 10 to 12 minutes, until the mixture thickens and coats the back of a wooden spoon. Remove from the heat and stir until the mixture cools just slightly. Stir in the butter, a piece at a time, until fully incorporated. Add the rind. Let cool completely.

2. Pour the cooled lemon curd into the baked shell(s) and chill until set.

VARIATIONS: Flavorful curds can be made from all citrus fruits. To make lime curd, substitute freshly squeezed lime juice for the lemon juice and increase the grated lime rind to 2 tablespoons. For orange curd, use the grated rind of 2 bright-skinned oranges and decrease the sugar to ⅔ cup.

Citrus Curd Tarts & Tartlets

Citrus curd tartlets can be topped with many different fruits. Here, they are topped with star fruit, pomegranate seeds, persimmons, and citrus zest. The tartlets are served on saucers from my set of Black Knight Bavarian china.

By modifying the basic recipe for Lemon Curd on page 95, you can create lime curd and orange curd, which are equally good fillings for small sweet-crust tarts and tartlets.

We catered a Southwest-style dinner party during the summer—lots of grilled quail and ribs, red-pepper glazed chicken, chili powder-and-lime-basted corn on the cob, corn bread, and flank steak. For dessert, we chose to serve citrus curd tarts. They are rich but not heavy, sweet but tart, and each variation is distinctive in flavor. To accentuate the flavors, we decorated the lemon tarts with a twist of fresh lemon slice, the orange tarts with candied strips of orange peel, and the lime tarts with candied lime slices.

Lemon, lime, and orange curd tarts served on my daughter Alexis' Fiestaware plates.

Every year from December through February, I buy boxes of clementines. These small tangerine-orange-like fruits are most frequently grown in Israel or Spain. They are thin-skinned and bright orange in color, and are often shipped to the United States with stems and leaves intact. The fruits are mostly seedless in character, as well as juicy and fragrant. Thinly sliced pieces cook well in a sugar syrup and make a candy-like dessert. Atop a custard, these slices bake to a lovely deep orange color and add flavor and interest to the tart. If placed carefully on the custard before baking, the slices do not sink, but remain afloat on top.

Candied clementine slices decorate the top of a tart served on early nineteenth-century Oriental patterned china. The table is covered with a Japanese obi cloth.

Candied Clementine Tart

THE RECIPE

Makes one 8½-inch tart

ONE 8½-INCH PÂTE BRISÉE TART SHELL (PAGE 198), PARTIALLY BAKED AND COOLED

- **4 EGGS, LIGHTLY BEATEN**
- **1 CUP GRANULATED SUGAR**
- **⅔ CUP FRESHLY SQUEEZED LEMON JUICE**
- **⅓ CUP FRESHLY SQUEEZED ORANGE JUICE**
- **GRATED RIND OF 1 LEMON AND 1 LARGE BRIGHT-SKINNED ORANGE**
- **¼ CUP HEAVY CREAM**
- **CANDIED CLEMENTINE SLICES (PAGE 100)**

1. Preheat the oven to 375°.

2. To make the filling, combine the eggs, sugar, lemon and orange juice and rind, and cream in a large mixing bowl, and whisk by hand for about 1 minute, until well blended. Pour the mixture into the partially baked tart shell. Gently place the candied clementine slices on the filling, around the perimeter of the tart, with sides just touching. Bake for 25 to 30 minutes, or until the filling is set and the top of the tart (and the clementines) is lightly browned. Let cool before serving.

Lemons, oranges, clementines, and limes can be stripped with a zester to create long strips of peel, which can then be cooked in a sugar syrup until glazed and crystalline. Slices of the same fruits can be slowly cooked in the same syrup until candied. Both the strips and the slices should be removed carefully from the hot syrup with a fork or slotted spoon and cooled on parchment paper until slightly hardened and dry. They can then be rolled in granulated sugar for a crunchier texture. The strips and slices can be stored in airtight containers in the freezer for future use.

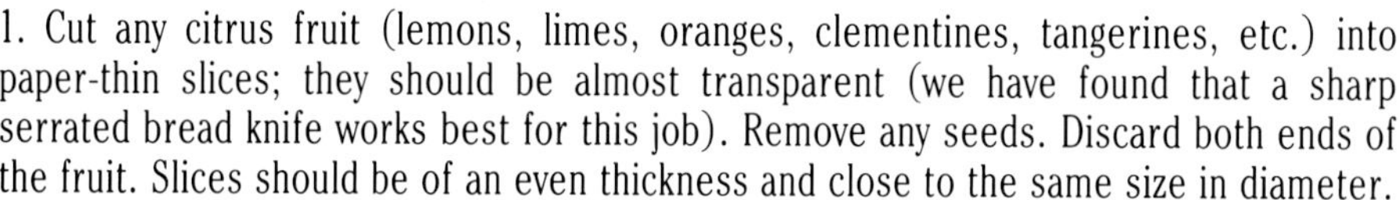

1. Cut any citrus fruit (lemons, limes, oranges, clementines, tangerines, etc.) into paper-thin slices; they should be almost transparent (we have found that a sharp serrated bread knife works best for this job). Remove any seeds. Discard both ends of the fruit. Slices should be of an even thickness and close to the same size in diameter.

2. In a large, heavy skillet or sauté pan, combine 2 cups granulated sugar and 1 cup water and bring to a rolling boil. Do not stir the syrup mixture or it may become cloudy; shake the pan to help the sugar dissolve. Lower the heat to a simmer when the liquid is clear and bubbly, and add the citrus slices in a single layer. Cook the fruit for 20 to 40 minutes with the syrup barely simmering. Be careful not to boil the fruit, or the pulp may fall away from the peel and disintegrate.

3. When the fruit slices have cooked and softened, very gently remove them from the syrup with a slotted spoon or flat spatula, and place on a parchment-lined baking sheet to cool.

VARIATION: Add 2 tablespoons Grand Marnier, Cointreau, or Triple Sec to the syrup when cooking the citrus slices.

Candied Citrus Peel

1. Using a stripper—a tool similar to a zester, but one which cuts a wider strip—or a very sharp paring knife, remove the rind *only* from any citrus fruit. Do not peel off any of the bitter white pith.

2. In a small heavy saucepan, combine 2 cups granulated sugar and ⅔ cup water. Bring to a slow rolling boil, lower the heat to simmer, add the citrus strips, and cook for about 40 minutes. Let the mixture cool and then remove the peelings from the syrup. Let harden on wax paper, parchment, or aluminum foil.

3. Candied citrus peel can be stored, tightly covered, in the freezer indefinitely.

VARIATION: Two tablespoons of any orange-flavored liqueur (Cointreau, Grand Marnier, or Triple Sec) can be stirred into the syrup after it is removed from the heat.

Key Lime Meringue Pie (left) *and Key Lime Pie* (right).

I am always on the lookout for the best Key lime pie, and whenever I spot this delicacy on a menu, I order it. My cousin Connie Kostyra lives in Miami and is another aficionado. Rarely does a month go by without a new recipe or two from her in the mail.

The main ingredient for this pie is the small, yellowish lime which is indigenous to the Florida Keys. This kind of lime is also grown in Mexico and in parts of the Southwest. Its mild, delicate fragrance and flavor is very different from that of the common, dark green Persian limes we can buy at the supermarket. Both recipes given here can be made with Persian limes, but the pies will have a more pungent, more tart taste.

The Key Lime Meringue Pie uses a pâte brisée crust, and the filling contains sweetened condensed milk, which many say must be in Key lime pie if it is to be considered the real thing. Key Lime Pie uses a graham cracker crust and is very similar to one of my favorite versions of this pie, the one served at Joe's Stone Crab Restaurant in Miami Beach. No amount of coaxing can get Joe's to reveal the restaurant's secret recipe.

Key Lime Meringue Pie

T H E R E C I P E

Makes one 8-inch pie

ONE 8-INCH PÂTE BRISÉE PIE SHELL (PAGE 198), BAKED AND COOLED

- 1 CAN (14 OUNCES) OF SWEETENED CONDENSED MILK
- 4 EGG YOLKS
- ½ CUP FRESH KEY LIME JUICE
- 1½ TABLESPOONS GRATED KEY LIME RIND
- 1 EGG WHITE, STIFFLY BEATEN
- ¼ TEASPOON CREAM OF TARTAR
- 5 EGG WHITES
- 6 TO 8 TABLESPOONS GRANULATED SUGAR

1. Preheat the oven to 375°.

2. In a mixing bowl, combine the sweetened condensed milk, egg yolks, lime juice, and rind. Gently fold the egg white into the mixture. Pour into the prepared crust.

3. To make the meringue, beat the egg whites with the cream of tartar until fluffy. Continue beating, and very gradually add the sugar. Beat for 7 to 8 minutes, to stiff peaks. Smooth the meringue over the filling, covering the filling completely and drawing the meringue to the crust. Bake for approximately 8 to 10 minutes, until the meringue is golden brown. Serve at room temperature—do not chill.

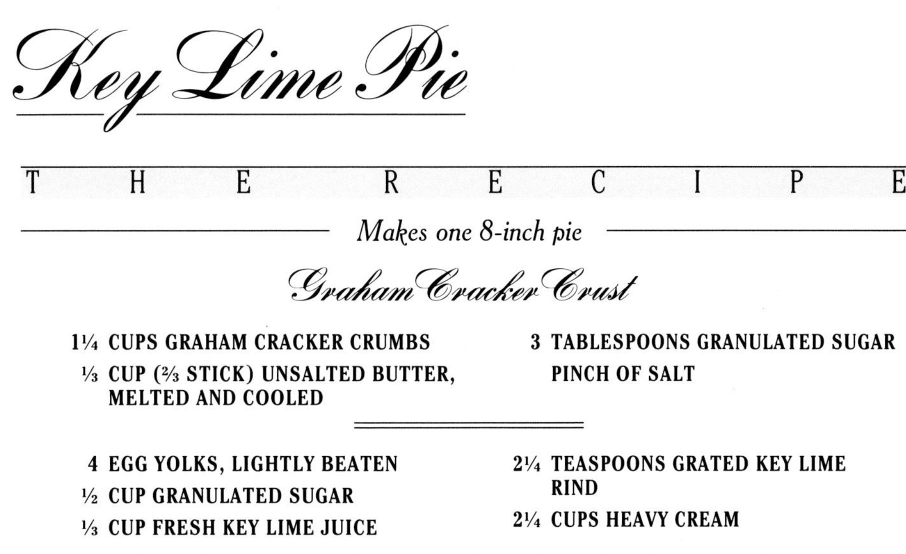

Key Lime Pie

T H E R E C I P E

Makes one 8-inch pie

Graham Cracker Crust

- 1¼ CUPS GRAHAM CRACKER CRUMBS
- ⅓ CUP (⅔ STICK) UNSALTED BUTTER, MELTED AND COOLED
- 3 TABLESPOONS GRANULATED SUGAR
- PINCH OF SALT

- 4 EGG YOLKS, LIGHTLY BEATEN
- ½ CUP GRANULATED SUGAR
- ⅓ CUP FRESH KEY LIME JUICE
- 2¼ TEASPOONS GRATED KEY LIME RIND
- 2¼ CUPS HEAVY CREAM

1. Preheat the oven to 375°. Combine all ingredients for the crust and mix well. Press into a buttered 8-inch pie plate and bake for about 15 minutes, until lightly browned. Let cool completely on a rack.

2. In the top of a double boiler, combine the egg yolks, sugar, and lime juice. Cook the mixture over moderate heat for about 10 minutes, until it coats the back of a spoon. Remove from the heat and stir in the grated rind. Chill until the mixture thickens, but do not let it become stiff.

3. Whip 1½ cups cream to soft peaks and fold it into the lime filling. Spoon into the baked crumb crust and chill, covered, for 24 hours. To serve, whip the remaining cream and pipe it onto the filling.

C H A P T E R

THE PIES AND TARTS IN THIS chapter—using more unusual fruits like figs, rhubarb, sour cherries, Concord grapes, papayas, kiwis, and persimmons—are some of my personal favorites, and I couldn't do a book without including them.

The Concord grape, sour cherry, and rhubarb pies are fabulous old-fashioned pies that disappear quickly whenever I serve them. They are quite American in character: The rhubarb is subtly spiced and flavored with a bit of cardamom, nutmeg, and orange, and the cherry with a bit of lemon. I don't add spices to the grape pie because the tart-sweet flavor of the Concord grapes is important enough by itself.

Delicate pâte brisée or puff pastry crusts or even nut crusts are used in making these tarts and tartlets. Citrus curd fillings, pastry cream, and jelly glazes accentuate the flavors and create glistening, jewel-like desserts.

Other fresh fruits and berries can be substituted for some of the harder-to-find or seasonal fruits, but always keep in mind that they must be perfect, ripe, and sweet. These pies and tarts are like beautiful showcases—anything less than perfection will not do.

Other Fruits

A nut crust is an excellent alternative to pâte brisée and is especially easy to make with a food processor. No rolling is necessary; the dough is simply pressed into a tart pan with the fingertips, baked, and then filled with fruits or berries. Another nice feature is that tarts made with a nut crust can be cut into wedges easily, without much crumbling. This fresh fig tart calls for a walnut crust, but an equally delicious crust could be made with almonds, filberts, pecans, or macadamia nuts.

We used the small California variety of green fig and the slightly larger violet-black type (Celeste) in these tarts. The honey-lemon glaze, spooned over the figs and enhanced by a sprinkle of freshly ground pepper and sautéed walnuts, is delicious.

These deep nut crusts, holding fillings of green and purple domestic figs, rest on an old wire cooling rack in front of our red barn.

Fig Tarts in Walnut Crust

T H E R E C I P E

Makes one deep 8½-inch tart

ONE DEEP 8½-INCH WALNUT CRUST TART SHELL (PAGE 205), BAKED AND COOLED

3 TABLESPOONS UNSALTED BUTTER
2 TABLESPOONS GRANULATED SUGAR
12 TO 16 FIRM RIPE UNBLEMISHED FRESH FIGS (GREEN OR PURPLE)

GLAZE: ½ CUP HONEY
JUICE OF ½ LEMON

GARNISH: 2 TABLESPOONS WALNUT HALVES SAUTÉED IN 1 TABLESPOON UNSALTED BUTTER
¼ TEASPOON COARSELY GROUND BLACK PEPPER

1. Preheat the oven to 400°. Use 1 tablespoon butter to coat a shallow baking dish large enough to hold all the figs. Place the figs in the pan, sprinkle with sugar, and bake for 8 to 12 minutes, until the fruit is soft. Let cool.

2. To make the glaze, combine the honey and lemon juice in a heavy saucepan. Bring to a boil and cook the mixture for 2 to 3 minutes, until it thickens. Stir in the remaining 2 tablespoons butter and continue to cook until the mixture is very thick and caramel-like. Keep warm over a pan of hot water.

3. To assemble the tart, place the cooked figs, stem ends up, in the tart shell. Spoon the glaze over the figs and garnish with the sautéed walnuts. Sprinkle with pepper. Serve at room temperature.

Papaya Tart

At right: *The unglazed tart.*
Below: *The tart glistens with its coating of apricot glaze.*

Jane Stacey made this tart many times for dinner and dessert parties when she worked in our catering kitchen. I have always loved papayas, an unusual tropical fruit with unique growing habits. The bulbous greenish fruit, which ripen to a deep golden yellow, grow straight from the trunk of the tree. The leaves of the tree grow out above the fruit like an umbrella, offering them shade and protection. If you live in a climate hospitable to papayas, you should try to grow them, because one tree can provide enough fruit for a family almost all year long.

Papayas are best when picked ripe from the tree, but since most fruits are shipped green to American markets, it is of utmost importance to ripen them at room temperature until fragrant, golden, and soft.

This tart should be assembled no more than two hours before serving. The papayas tend to crack and become a bit watery if they are sliced too far in advance.

T H E   R E C I P E

Makes one 11½-inch tart

ONE 11½-INCH PÂTE BRISÉE TART SHELL (PAGE 198), BAKED AND COOLED

3 TO 4 LARGE UNBLEMISHED RIPE PAPAYAS

1 CUP CRÈME PÂTISSIÈRE (PAGE 63)

1 CUP WARM APRICOT GLAZE (PAGE 211)

1. Peel the papayas with a sharp vegetable peeler, halve them, scoop out the black seeds, and cut the fruit lengthwise into slices ⅛ inch thick using a very sharp knife.

2. Spoon the pastry cream evenly into the tart shell. Carefully arrange the papaya slices in overlapping rows on the pastry cream, covering it completely. Brush lightly with the apricot glaze. Let cool before serving.

Jane's Concord Grape Pie

Some time ago we were asked to cater a luncheon for the King and Queen of Sweden, who were visiting New York on official business. We were told that the menu should reflect the "New American Cuisine," and that, if possible, only American ingredients be used. I proposed the Concord grape pie as dessert, because it was unusual yet typically American.

Four of us spent a total of nine hours seeding Concord grapes, a tedious task. Each grape was cut in half, and the seeds removed with the fingernails or with the point of a knife. After the grapes were seeded, making the pies was relatively easy.

The royal couple loved the pie. But when Queen Silvia smiled to thank us, I noticed that her teeth matched the color of her periwinkle-blue dress and hat! I vowed that from then on I would serve this spectacular pie only in the evening, by candlelight.

The crust of this pie was deeply crimped, and it was garnished with a cluster of pastry grapes, including leaves and tendrils.

THE RECIPE

Makes one 8-inch pie

ONE 11-INCH CIRCLE OF PÂTE BRISÉE (PAGE 198), CHILLED

3 POUNDS (APPROXIMATELY 2 QUARTS) CONCORD GRAPES

1 CUP GRANULATED SUGAR

¾ CUP CORNSTARCH

GLAZE: 1 EGG BEATEN WITH 1 TABLESPOON HEAVY CREAM

1. Preheat the oven to 400°. Line an 8-inch pie plate with the pastry. Trim the edges and crimp as desired. Chill. Roll out the pastry scraps and with a sharp paring knife cut out a bunch of grapes and individual leaf shapes. Delineate individual grapes and the veins of the leaves using the back of the knife. Place on wax paper and chill.

2. Wash, halve, and pit the grapes, reserving the juice that results. Strain the grape juice and measure out ¾ cup.

3. In a medium saucepan, combine the grape juice, sugar, and cornstarch. Bring the mixture to a boil and cook for 2 to 3 minutes, stirring constantly. Remove from the heat, stir in the grapes, and let cool.

4. When the grape filling is completely cooled, pour it into the pie shell. Place the grape cutouts directly on top of the filling and arrange the "leaves" as desired. (We also created a "grapevine" by twisting a long, narrow pastry scrap and placing it on top.) Brush the crimped edges and the top pastry decorations with the egg glaze. Bake for approximately 40 minutes, or until the grape juice is thick and bubbling at the center of the pie. Let cool completely before serving.

Three grape tarts are served with tea from a beautiful green celadon Japanese lustre tea set. Huge flowering kales provide an interesting table decoration.

Three different varieties of grapes and three different glazes were used for these tarts. We glazed green seedless Thompson grapes with crab apple jelly; red seedless King Ruby grapes with quince; and black-purple Ribier grapes, which must be seeded for use in tarts, with red currant. Glazes add not only sparkling color but also extra flavor to tarts made with fruit fillings.

Grape Tarts in Almond Nut Crust

THE RECIPE

Makes one 7½-inch tart

ONE 7½-INCH ALMOND NUT CRUST TART SHELL (PAGE 205), BAKED AND COOLED

1½ POUNDS SEEDLESS GREEN (THOMPSON), SEEDLESS RED (KING RUBY), OR BLACK (RIBIER) GRAPES

1 CUP CRAB APPLE, QUINCE, OR RED CURRANT GLAZE (PAGE 211)

Wash, halve, and seed the grapes. Arrange them, cut sides down, in concentric circles on the nut crust. Carefully place another layer of grapes on top of the first layer. Brush lightly with the appropriate glaze. Refrigerate for at least an hour before serving.

NOTE: We used glazes to complement the color of the grapes: crab apple jelly glaze for green grapes, quince for red grapes, and red currant for black grapes.

Each June we pick gallons and gallons of sour cherries. We try to get to them before the birds do, and have even devised a set of net coverings to protect the cherries. Our four Montmorency trees give us more than enough cherries for eating out of hand, for the freezer, and for sour cherry jelly, which has become my favorite glaze for fruit tarts.

My brother George was born on February 22, and his traditional birthday cake has always been a sour cherry pie. I think I planted the cherry trees just to always have a supply of pitted sour cherries in the freezer for use in February. We pit the cherries as soon as they are picked—we have not yet found a cherry pitter that works better than our fingers—and immediately pack them in quart quantities in plastic bags for the freezer. The faster all of the picking, pitting, and freezing is done, the less likely the cherries will darken or bruise. I never use any sugar on the pitted cherries; I just freeze them in their natural state, along with all the juice. To use the frozen berries, I thaw them in the refrigerator overnight, or at room temperature, right in the plastic bags.

This pie was baked in a large earthenware platter designed by Andy's sister, Diane Love. The lattice strips and decorative pastry leaves were cut out with a pastry wheel.

Sour Cherry Pie

T H E R E C I P E

Makes one 15-inch double-crust pie

ONE UNBAKED 15-INCH PÂTE BRISÉE PIE SHELL PLUS ADDITIONAL PASTRY FOR THE LATTICE AND LEAVES, CHILLED (YOU WILL NEED TO DOUBLE THE BASIC RECIPE ON PAGE 198)

- **8 CUPS PITTED SOUR CHERRIES PLUS 1 CUP RESERVED CHERRY JUICE**
- **2 CUPS GRANULATED SUGAR, OR TO TASTE**
- **2 TABLESPOONS ALL-PURPOSE FLOUR**
- **5 TABLESPOONS CORNSTARCH**
- **JUICE AND GRATED RIND OF 1 LARGE LEMON**
- **4 TABLESPOONS (½ STICK) COLD UNSALTED BUTTER, CUT INTO SMALL PIECES**

GLAZE: 1 EGG BEATEN WITH 2 TABLESPOONS HEAVY CREAM

1. Preheat the oven to 400°.

2. Put the sour cherries and juice in a large mixing bowl and sprinkle in the sugar, flour, cornstarch, and lemon juice and rind. Toss well and pour into the pastry shell. Dot with butter and weave the lattice top over the filling. Brush the lattice and the edges of the pastry with the egg glaze and bake for approximately 1¼ hours, until the pastry is golden and the juices in the center of the pie are bubbling. Let cool slightly before cutting.

NOTE: The filling ingredients can be halved to make a 9-inch pie. Reduce the baking time to approximately 50 minutes.

A mixture of whipped cream and lemon curd fills a puff pastry tartlet shell topped with slices of persimmon.

Persimmon Tartlets with Lemon Cream Filling

Andy and I went to the big island of Hawaii recently for a vacation of water sports and hiking. While exploring the island's hidden valleys, we came upon the little-known, virtually uninhabited valley of the Waipio. On our day-long hike through this enchanted place, we came upon an abandoned orchard. We had been told that every kind of tropical fruit could be found in this orchard, and on that day we discovered the joy of eating truly tree-ripened fruits of such variety and perfection that we were to be spoiled forever.

There were orange-yellow loquats, giant Japanese grapefruit, and tangerines, tangelos, guavas, papayas, cherimoyas, mangoes, soursops, and breadfruit, among others. The most wonderful, to me, were the perfectly ripe persimmons, which were just falling off the tree. I have never found persimmons in the fruit markets so fine as those in the Waipio, but if you shop carefully, very good persimmons can be found and ripened at home on the kitchen counter. When ready to use, the persimmon has none of the tart, mouth-tightening unpleasantness of unripe fruit. The flesh is soft yet firm, the skin totally edible, and the color a dark orangy red.

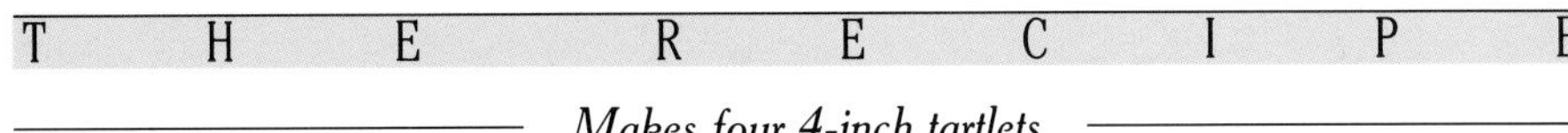

THE RECIPE

Makes four 4-inch tartlets

½ POUND PUFF PASTRY (PAGE 206), CHILLED

¼ CUP HEAVY CREAM
½ CUP LEMON CURD (PAGE 95)

2 UNBRUISED BUT RIPE PERSIMMONS, CUT LENGTHWISE INTO SLICES ⅛ INCH THICK

1. Roll out the puff pastry to a thickness of ⅛ inch. Using a 4-inch tart ring with a sharp bottom edge or a large biscuit cutter, cut 8 rounds of pastry. Then using a 3½-inch ring, cut 4 of the rounds into smaller rounds, centering the ring so that an even rim is produced. Paste the rims onto the larger rounds at the outside edge with a bit of water, carefully aligning the edges; this forms a raised border on the tartlet. Place the pastry on a parchment-lined or water-sprayed baking sheet and chill for at least 30 minutes.

2. Preheat the oven to 400°. Prick the bottom of each pastry, line with foil, and weight, as described on page 208. Bake the rounds for approximately 10 to 15 minutes, until they are puffed and golden brown. Let cool completely on a rack before filling.

3. Whip the cream to soft peaks and gently fold it into the lemon curd. Mound ¼ cup of the mixture in each tartlet shell. Top each with a slice or two of persimmon, and serve immediately.

VARIATION: Substitute mashed persimmon pulp for the lemon curd. Fold in the whipped cream and proceed as above.

When we baked this wide-lattice rhubarb pie (the lattice was cut with a pastry wheel), it reminded me of a beautiful tartan plaid.

This is an extraordinarily good pie, and a fabulous way to use up excess rhubarb from the garden. My favorite variety of rhubarb to grow is Valentine, the reddest and sweetest of all the red rhubarbs.

The addition of cardamom, nutmeg, orange juice, and orange zest perks up the rhubarb's natural tartness. It is very easy to eat several pieces of this pie!

Tartan Rhubarb Pie

T H E R E C I P E

Makes one 12-inch double-crust pie

TWO 13-INCH CIRCLES OF PÂTE BRISÉE (PAGE 198), CHILLED

- 2½ POUNDS FRESH RHUBARB, CUT INTO ½-INCH PIECES, OR TWO 20-OUNCE PACKAGES OF FROZEN RHUBARB, THAWED
- 1 CUP GRANULATED SUGAR, OR TO TASTE
- ½ CUP ALL-PURPOSE FLOUR
- 1 SCANT TABLESPOON GROUND CARDAMOM
- 1 TEASPOON FRESHLY GRATED NUTMEG
- JUICE AND GRATED RIND OF 1 BRIGHT-SKINNED ORANGE

1. Preheat the oven to 375°. Line a 12-inch pie plate with one round, leaving the excess pastry to hang over, and chill. Using a pastry wheel, cut as many 3- to 4-inch-wide strips as possible from the other round for the lattice top. Place on a parchment-lined or water-sprayed baking sheet and chill for at least 30 minutes.

2. Put the rhubarb in a large mixing bowl. Combine the remaining ingredients in another bowl. Sprinkle this mixture over the rhubarb and stir to coat all the fruit. Turn the fruit into the prepared crust. Weave the lattice strips over the filling, securing the ends by pasting them to the crust with a bit of water. Turn up the overhang of the bottom crust, trim, and crimp as desired. Bake for approximately 50 minutes, until the filling has bubbled and thickened. Let cool before serving.

NOTE: If you use frozen rhubarb, be sure it is completely thawed and well drained.

Kiwi Flamboyancy

I love this little odd fruit from New Zealand. The woolly skin encloses a green sweet-sour flesh that tastes like a cross between a lime, an apple, and a strawberry. If used when perfectly ripe and unblemished, slices of kiwi make lovely toppings for tarts. I call this creation Kiwi Flamboyancy since the bright green tart, when surrounded with a lei of full-blown pink roses, is a rather extraordinary sight.

The kiwi fruit must be peeled with a sharp vegetable peeler or knife. It can be sliced lengthwise, as illustrated, or crosswise, or cut into quarters or eighths. The small black seeds are perfectly edible, and actually enhance the appearance of the fruit.

Slices of kiwi fruit are arranged on top of a pastry cream filling and then glazed with sour cherry jelly. The roses are from a Queen Elizabeth hybrid tea bush, the longest lived rosebush in our garden.

T H E R E C I P E

Makes one 7½-inch tart

ONE 7½-INCH PÂTE BRISÉE TART SHELL (PAGE 198), BAKED AND COOLED

⅓ CUP CRÈME PÂTISSIÈRE (PAGE 63)

5 FIRM BUT RIPE KIWIS, PEELED AND THINLY SLICED LENGTHWISE

GLAZE: ⅓ CUP SOUR CHERRY JELLY (PAGE 211), MELTED AND STRAINED

Spread the crème pâtissière evenly in the bottom of the tart shell. Arrange the kiwi slices on top in overlapping rows. Brush lightly with the melted jelly. Let cool before serving.

CHAPTER 7.

ALMOST ANY VEGETABLE CAN BE used as a sweet pie filling if you use your imagination and lots of sugar and spices. Many different cultures use vegetables in sweet desserts. The recipes in this chapter are some of my favorites. They are not too complex, nor are they difficult to prepare, but they do call for fresh ingredients, many of which need advance preparation and cooking—so you will need to plan accordingly.

I love all kinds of squashes for pie fillings—acorn, butternut, Hubbard, and Turk's Turbans—and find I can vary the taste of each with different spices and sweeteners—honey, molasses, brown or white sugar, and cinnamon, mace, nutmeg, ginger, or allspice. Sweet potatoes, green tomatoes, beets, spinach, carrots, and parsnips all make excellent fillings, too. We grow everything used in these pies except the sweet potatoes, which don't seem to grow well in Connecticut. I grow sugar pumpkins for extra-sweet pumpkin flesh and large red beets, which are baked until tender in a foil envelope and then peeled for use. The carrots and parsnips are best in autumn and winter, after they have had a bit of frost to sweeten them.

Several of these pies could be used in the small tartlet size to accompany roasts as part of the main course. The beet pie would be wonderful with roast pork, and the carrot-parsnip pie would go well with veal. (If you want to serve a sweet pie as a savory, be sure to reduce the amount of sugar by one-third to one-half, increase the salt, and add pepper.)

Vegetables

Alexis' Sweet Potato Pie

Ever since my first visit to Sylvia's, one of Harlem's great family-style restaurants, I've loved sweet potato pie. Now, when I visit the South or the home of a southern friend, I often ask for this pie. Chef Paul Prudhomme makes a great sweet potato pecan pie, and the Belle Meade Hotel in Nashville doesn't do too badly either.

My daughter Alexis' recipe is the one I use at home whenever I find extra-plump, unblemished sweet potatoes at the market. Her recipe is the result of much tasting and testing. She loves Sylvia's pie, but prefers it less sweet. And she doesn't care for pecans, which she thinks detract from the purity of the potato taste.

A well-made pie of sweet potatoes is dense but not overly heavy. It is not sickly sweet and should not resemble candied sweet potatoes or marshmallowed yams in any way. The potatoes must be boiled or baked until tender, then peeled and mashed by hand so the filling has texture. It should not be a smooth custard like pumpkin or squash pie.

THE RECIPE

Makes one 9-inch pie

ONE UNBAKED 9-INCH PÂTE BRISÉE PIE SHELL (PAGE 198), CHILLED

- 4 MEDIUM-SIZE SWEET POTATOES, COOKED UNTIL SOFT AND PEELED
- 3 EGGS, LIGHTLY BEATEN
- ⅓ CUP GRANULATED SUGAR
- ¼ TEASPOON FRESHLY GRATED NUTMEG
- ¾ TEASPOON CINNAMON
- ½ TEASPOON ALLSPICE
- ¼ TEASPOON SALT
- 1 TEASPOON GRATED LEMON RIND
- 1½ CUPS LIGHT CREAM
- 4 TABLESPOONS (½ STICK) UNSALTED BUTTER, MELTED AND COOLED

1. Preheat the oven to 400°.

2. Put the sweet potatoes in a large mixing bowl and mash with a wooden spoon or a potato masher. Set aside.

3. Combine the eggs, sugar, spices, salt, lemon rind, and cream in a small bowl and whisk until combined. Pour this mixture into the sweet potatoes and stir until thoroughly combined. Add the butter and mix well. Pour into the pie crust and bake for 45 to 55 minutes, or until the filling is set and a knife inserted in the center comes out clean. Let cool completely before slicing.

7

A luscious sweet potato pie with a fork-marked crust. The Fiestaware dishes and Bakelite cutlery were loaned to me by the Friedman Gallery in Westport, which specializes in Art Deco and Art Yukko.

Cooked beets are grated and mixed with a rich sweet custard to make the filling for this pie. There are several ways to cook beets. One is to wrap the unpeeled beets in foil and bake them in a 350° oven until tender; another is to boil the unpeeled beets in water until tender. (A pressure cooker is also very quick and efficient.) The skins should slip off the beets quite easily once they are cooked and cooled. For such a small amount, it is simple to grate the beets by hand, but a food processor saves your fingers from beet-red stains. I always wear thin rubber gloves when peeling or grating beets because otherwise my fingers retain the color for days.

In France and elsewhere in Europe it is a common practice to sell precooked beets in the vegetable markets, which I think is a good idea. We would probably use this delicious vegetable more if the cooking and peeling weren't such a chore.

Beet Pie

T H E R E C I P E

Makes one 10½-inch pie

ONE UNBAKED 10½-INCH PÂTE BRISÉE PIE SHELL (PAGE 198), WELL CHILLED

- 2 POUNDS FRESH BEETS
- ½ TEASPOON FRESHLY GRATED NUTMEG
- 1¼ CUPS HEAVY CREAM
- 1¼ CUPS MILK
- ½ VANILLA BEAN
- ½ CUP GRANULATED SUGAR
- 3 WHOLE EGGS PLUS 3 EGG YOLKS, LIGHTLY BEATEN

1. Cut the tops off the beets, leaving 1 inch of stem. Wash the beets, put them in a large pot, cover with water, and bring to a boil. Cook the beets, covered, until they are tender, adding more boiling water as needed. Remove the cooked beets from the water and let cool.

2. When the beets are cool enough to handle, slip off the skins and coarsely grate them by hand or in a food processor. Stir in the nutmeg and set aside.

3. Preheat the oven to 350°.

4. Combine the cream, milk, and vanilla bean in a heavy saucepan and let simmer for 5 minutes. Remove the vanilla bean.

5. Using an electric mixer, beat the sugar with the eggs and egg yolks until light and fluffy. Gradually add the hot cream-milk mixture, beating constantly. Strain the mixture into a large mixing bowl and stir in the grated beets, mixing well. Pour into the pie shell and bake for approximately 55 to 60 minutes, until the filling is set and the pastry evenly browned. Let cool a bit before cutting. Serve warm or at room temperature.

I decorated this beet pie with an applied braided edge of pâte brisée. A wedge of it is served on an old French pink lustre plate on top of a Japanese obi table runner.

Sweet Spinach Pie

This pie was photographed in our February greenhouse, where we grow baby spinach, lettuce, and herbs.

Like the beet pie, this pie has a custard filling. The combination of spinach with pignolia nuts and apples is unusual but very good, especially when nutmeg and cloves are added. This dessert was baked as an open-faced pie with a sprinkling of sugar, but a lattice top would be attractive, too, as would a leaf-decorated topping.

THE RECIPE

Makes one 11-inch pie

ONE UNBAKED 11-INCH PÂTE BRISÉE PIE SHELL (PAGE 198), WELL CHILLED

2 POUNDS FRESH SPINACH, WASHED AND STEMS REMOVED

⅔ CUP PIGNOLIA NUTS

1¼ CUPS HEAVY CREAM

1¼ CUPS MILK

½ VANILLA BEAN

½ CUP PLUS 1 TABLESPOON GRANULATED SUGAR

3 WHOLE EGGS PLUS 3 EGG YOLKS, LIGHTLY BEATEN

3 MEDIUM-SIZE TART APPLES, PEELED, CORED, AND THINLY SLICED

¼ TEASPOON FRESHLY GRATED NUTMEG

PINCH OF GROUND CLOVES

1. Steam the spinach leaves over boiling water for 3 to 4 minutes, until wilted but still bright green. Remove from the heat, pat dry, and when cool enough to handle, chop coarsely. Set aside.

2. Preheat the oven to 350°.

3. Spread the nuts in a single layer on a baking sheet and bake for approximately 10 minutes, until the nuts are lightly toasted. Let cool.

4. Combine the cream, milk, and vanilla bean in a heavy saucepan and let simmer for 5 minutes. Remove the vanilla bean.

5. Using an electric mixer, beat ½ cup sugar with the eggs and egg yolks until light and fluffy. Add the hot cream-milk mixture in a slow steady stream, beating continually. Strain the mixture into a large mixing bowl and stir in the spinach, apples, nuts, nutmeg, and cloves. Pour into the pie shell, sprinkle the remaining 1 tablespoon sugar on top, and bake for 55 to 60 minutes, until the filling is set and the pastry evenly browned. Let cool a bit before cutting. Serve warm or at room temperature.

VARIATION: For a more savory spinach pie, substitute a large pinch of cayenne pepper for the tablespoon sugar sprinkled on top before baking.

Green Tomato Pie

Right: *Sliced green tomatoes sit for a while with raisins, vinegar, and lemon rind before baking.* Left: *The fully baked pie. The pastry has simply been folded over the filling.*

One summer in Nutley, when I was about four or five years old, I did a very bad thing. Many of our neighbors grew tomatoes and other things in Victory gardens on abandoned farmland behind our house. For some reason I cannot recall, I picked every single green tomato from every tomato plant in every garden. There was an appropriate uproar in the neighborhood, and I was duly punished (how I cannot remember). My mother had to come up with new ways to use these generally useless things—piccalili, green tomato mincemeat, pickled green tomatoes, fried green tomato slices, and green tomato pie.

Now, of course, I eat green tomatoes only in the autumn, when they have to be picked before the first blackening frost. It is then that I make my version of Mother's green tomato pie. I put the slices of tomato, mixed with raisins, lemon rind, and spices, in the bottom crust of a basic pâte brisée, fold the edges up over the filling, and bake the pie. It has an old-fashioned taste that I find irresistible.

T H E R E C I P E

Makes one 9-inch pie

ONE 14-INCH CIRCLE OF PÂTE BRISÉE (PAGE 198), CHILLED

6 MEDIUM-SIZE GREEN TOMATOES
¾ CUP GOLDEN RAISINS
1½ TEASPOONS GRATED LEMON RIND
2 TABLESPOONS LEMON JUICE
1 TABLESPOON CIDER VINEGAR
1½ CUPS GRANULATED SUGAR
4 TABLESPOONS ALL-PURPOSE FLOUR
SCANT ½ TEASPOON SALT
¼ TEASPOON CINNAMON
¼ TEASPOON GROUND GINGER
2 TABLESPOONS COLD UNSALTED BUTTER, CUT INTO SMALL PIECES
CONFECTIONERS' SUGAR

1. Center the pastry in a 9-inch pie plate (the overhang will be folded up over the filling). Chill.

2. Preheat the oven to 425°.

3. Wash the tomatoes and cut them into ⅛-inch-thick slices; discard the stem ends. Put the tomato slices in a large mixing bowl and add the raisins, lemon rind and juice, and vinegar. Stir and set aside.

4. Combine the sugar, flour, salt, and spices in a small bowl. Sprinkle 2 tablespoons of this mixture over the chilled pie crust and toss the rest with the sliced tomatoes. Turn the mixture into the pie crust and dot with butter. Fold the pastry up over the filling and bake for 15 minutes. Reduce the heat to 325° and bake for another 50 minutes, or until the filling is bubbling and the crust is golden brown.

5. Let the pie cool completely before cutting; the filling is very liquid and might be runny. Dust the top of the pie with confectioners' sugar immediately before serving.

For this pie the carrots and parsnips need only be peeled and grated before being added to the filling. Choose parsnips that are firm, not flaccid, and as creamy-colored as possible. Carrots should be crisp, bright orange, and sweet.

This is a custardlike pie. The cinnamon and nutmeg enhance the flavor of the carrots and parsnips and make these vegetables work well in a dessert. Either vegetable could have been used alone, but the combination is what makes the filling most interesting.

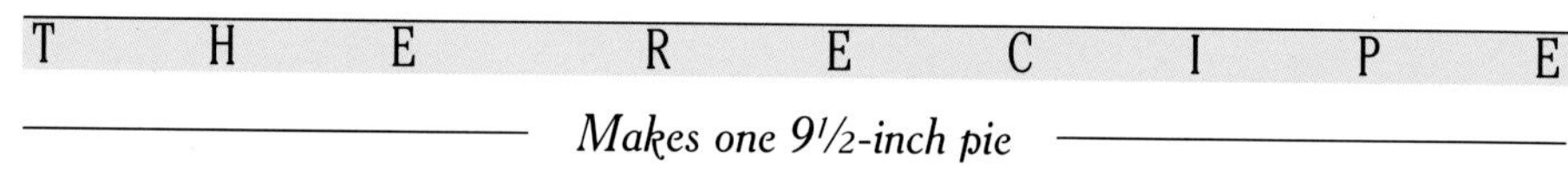

Carrot-Parsnip Pie

THE RECIPE

Makes one 9½-inch pie

ONE UNBAKED 9½-INCH PÂTE BRISÉE PIE SHELL (PAGE 198), CHILLED

- 3 EGGS, LIGHTLY BEATEN
- ⅓ CUP PACKED LIGHT BROWN SUGAR
- 3 TABLESPOONS GRANULATED SUGAR
- 1 CUP HEAVY CREAM
- ⅔ CUP MILK
- 2 TEASPOONS ALL-PURPOSE FLOUR
- 1 TEASPOON CINNAMON
- ½ TEASPOON FRESHLY GRATED NUTMEG
- 2 CUPS GRATED CARROTS
- 1 CUP GRATED PARSNIPS

Glazed Carrot Strips

- 2 CARROTS, PEELED
- 1 CUP WATER
- 6 TABLESPOONS GRANULATED SUGAR

1. Preheat the oven to 350°.

2. Put the eggs in a mixing bowl and stir in the sugars until well blended. Add the cream, milk, flour, cinnamon, and nutmeg, mixing until thoroughly blended. Stir in the carrots and parsnips.

3. Pour the filling into the pie shell and bake for 55 to 60 minutes, until set and lightly browned. Let cool completely on a wire rack.

4. To make the glazed carrot strips, peel long, ½-inch wide strips from the carrots, using a very sharp vegetable peeler. Put the strips in a heavy saucepan with the water and sugar and cook until the carrots are tender and glazed. Let cool completely in the syrup before garnishing the pie and serving.

A generous slice of carrot-parsnip pie, garnished with candied carrot strips, is served on a square English plate made in the 1930s.

c.

a.

b.

Each of these squash pies, shown just before baking, was made with pâte brisée, but the edges are all different: (a) *Spicy Butternut Squash Pie with a checkerboard edge,* (b) *Brown Sugar Pumpkin with an applied leaf edge,* (c) *Acorn Squash with a fine braided edge,* (d) *Golden Maple Pumpkin with a deep, distinctive fluting, and* (e) *Sugar Pumpkin Molasses with a very simple fluted edge.*

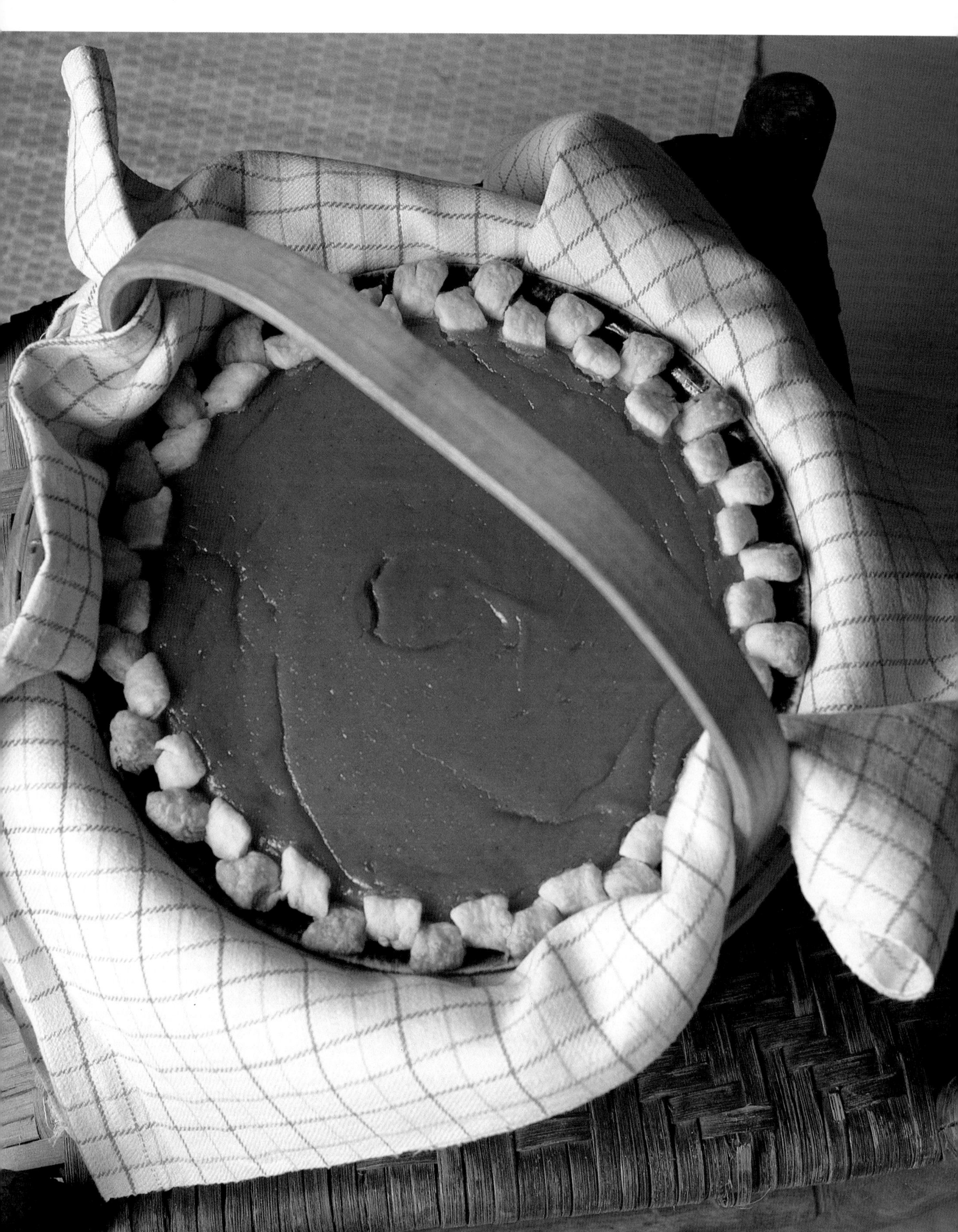

a Spicy Butternut Squash Pie

A checkerboard edge is a nice decoration for this plain-looking but delicious pie.

Butternut squash is a very popular winter squash. Cylindrical in shape, with a thick neck, small seed cavities in the bottom, and deep orange flesh, this type of squash is high in vitamin C. Butternut squash purée can be used in any pumpkin pie recipe, for it is quite similar in taste and texture. Butternut squashes are very good keepers, which means they can be stored in a cool, dry place for quite a long time. However, I find it easier to make lots of purée when the fruits are ripe in September and October and freeze it in two-cup amounts. That way I can make a pie whenever I want to, without going through the time-consuming process of preparing the squash.

The filling for this pie is thick and spicy, with a definite molasses flavor. The checkerboard pastry edge is easy to do —just snip the pastry at even intervals along the edge and bend every other section back toward the center of the pie.

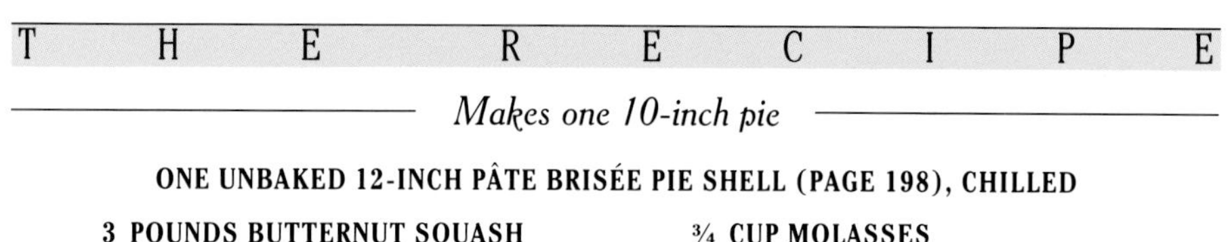

T H E R E C I P E

Makes one 10-inch pie

ONE UNBAKED 12-INCH PÂTE BRISÉE PIE SHELL (PAGE 198), CHILLED

3 POUNDS BUTTERNUT SQUASH
½ TEASPOON CINNAMON
1 TEASPOON GINGER
1 TEASPOON SALT
¾ CUP MOLASSES
5 EGGS, LIGHTLY BEATEN
¾ CUP HEAVY CREAM

1. To make the checkerboard edging, trim the pastry at the outer edge of the pie plate and cut the pastry ½ inch deep at ¾-inch intervals all around the edge. Bend every other section of the edging back into the pie plate. Chill until firm.

2. Halve the squash, remove the seeds, and cut it into large chunks. Put a wire rack in a large saucepan and add water to within 1 inch of the rack. Put the squash, cut sides up, on the rack, bring the water to a boil, lower the heat, and cook, covered, for 20 to 25 minutes, until the squash is tender. (You may need to add more boiling water to the pan.) Remove the squash and let cool.

3. Preheat the oven to 450°.

4. When the squash is cool enough to handle, scrape the flesh from the skin and put it in the bowl of a food processor. Purée until smooth. Spoon the purée into another bowl and mix in the spices, salt, and molasses. Add the eggs and the cream and blend thoroughly. Pour the filling into the pie crust and bake for 10 minutes. Lower the temperature to 350° and bake for another 45 minutes, or until the filling is set. Let cool slightly before serving.

This pie was baked in my favorite tin plate, the one with the hexagonal shape and wide sides. It is an excellent tin for making pies with decorative edgings.

We baked two pies using this recipe; in one we used a commercially prepared pumpkin purée for the filling, and in the other two cups of our own homemade purée. Both were excellent, but the store-bought pumpkin produced a very smooth pie. If a smooth glossy filling is desired it is important to put the pulp through a very fine sieve or food mill, or to process it until smooth in a food processor. I often process it first and then press it through a sieve to remove any fibers or lumps.

This brown sugar pumpkin pie, baked in a hexagonal tin, looks very special with the addition of pastry leaves around the edge.

6. Brown Sugar Pumpkin Pie

THE RECIPE

Makes one 8-inch pie

ONE 12-INCH CIRCLE OF PÂTE BRISÉE (PAGE 117), CHILLED

- **2 CUPS FRESH PUMPKIN PURÉE (PAGE 142) OR ONE 15-OUNCE CAN PUMPKIN PURÉE**
- **3 EGGS, LIGHTLY BEATEN**
- **½ CUP HEAVY CREAM**
- **½ CUP PACKED DARK BROWN SUGAR**
- **½ TEASPOON ALLSPICE**
- **½ TEASPOON CINNAMON**
- **½ TEASPOON GROUND GINGER**
- **½ TEASPOON SALT**

1. Preheat the oven to 375°.

2. Line an 8-inch pie plate with the rolled-out pastry and trim it even with the edge of the pie plate. Cut as many leaf shapes from the excess pastry as possible, and make vein markings in each leaf with the back of the knife. With a little water, attach the pastry leaves to the edge of the pie crust so that the leaves fall over the edge of the pie plate. Keep well chilled until ready to use.

3. Combine the purée with the remaining ingredients in a mixing bowl and stir until well blended. Pour into the prepared pastry and bake for 50 to 55 minutes, or until the crust is nicely browned and the custard set. Let cool before serving.

c. Acorn Squash Custard Pie

T H E R E C I P E

Makes one 8-inch pie

ONE 12-INCH CIRCLE OF PÂTE BRISÉE (PAGE 198), CHILLED

2 ACORN SQUASHES (APPROXIMATELY 3 TO 3½ POUNDS TOTAL)
4 EGGS, LIGHTLY BEATEN
½ CUP HONEY
¾ CUP HALF-AND-HALF
½ TEASPOON SALT
1 TEASPOON GROUND GINGER

1. Press the rolled-out pastry into an 8-inch pie plate. Trim it just over the lip of the pie plate with a sharp paring knife. Cut as many ¼-inch-wide strips as possible from the excess pastry. Braid together three strips at a time, securing them at the ends with a bit of water and gently pressing together. Attach this braid to the edge of the pastry with a small amount of water. Chill well.

2. Halve and seed the squashes and cut into large chunks. Put them in a steamer, skin sides down, and cook over boiling water for 20 to 30 minutes until tender. Let cool slightly before scraping the squash from its skin and puréeing it in the bowl of a food processor.

3. Preheat the oven to 375°.

4. Combine the puréed squash with the remaining ingredients and mix until well combined. Pour into the pie crust and bake for 1 hour, or until the custard is firm and the crust is golden brown. Let cool completely before cutting.

Acorn squash is a winter vegetable with a heavily ridged black-green shell and yellow or bright orange flesh. These squashes used to grow on long, long vines and took up a lot of space in the fall garden, but now there are wonderful "bush" varieties that produce numerous fruits on one compact plant. There is even a new variety that produces bright orange-skinned squashes!

This pie, with a honey-sweetened filling gently flavored with ginger, is the lightest of all the squash pies.

d. Golden Maple Pumpkin Pie

We fashioned a maple leaf from leftover pâte brisée to place on top of this pie as an edible garnish. The leaf was baked separately because it would have disappeared into the thin custard filling. (Cut the leaf shape from pastry scraps and bake in a preheated 375° oven for 12 to 15 minutes, until golden brown.)

Be sure to chill the crust well before filling with the custard, to ensure that the fluting remains defined after baking.

T H E R E C I P E

Makes one 11-inch pie

ONE UNBAKED 11-INCH PÂTE BRISÉE PIE SHELL (PAGE 198), WELL CHILLED

1½ CUPS FRESH PUMPKIN PURÉE (PAGE 142) OR CANNED PUMPKIN PURÉE
½ CUP MAPLE SYRUP
1½ CUPS MILK
2 EGGS, LIGHTLY BEATEN
2 TABLESPOONS ALL-PURPOSE FLOUR
1 TEASPOON CINNAMON
¼ TEASPOON FRESHLY GRATED NUTMEG
¼ TEASPOON GROUND GINGER
½ TEASPOON SALT

GARNISH: A PASTRY LEAF (BAKED AND COOLED)

1. Preheat the oven to 425°.

2. Put the pumpkin purée in a large bowl and add the syrup, milk, and eggs; mix until smooth. Stir in the dry ingredients and combine thoroughly. Pour the mixture into the pie shell and bake for approximately 40 minutes, until the filling is firm and a knife inserted in the center comes out clean. Let cool before serving. Garnish with a prebaked pastry leaf, if desired.

Acorn squash custard pie (right) topped with a real sycamore leaf, and golden maple pumpkin pie (left), which is garnished with a pâte brisée leaf.

VEGETABLES

e. Sugar Pumpkin Molasses Pie

Sugar pumpkins are small and uniform, usually only 6 to 7 inches in diameter. They are my favorite for pies because the flesh is sweet and thick, with a delicious flavor. Big Max pumpkins and French *potirons (jaune gros)* are fun for show, for soups, and for vegetable purées, but for pies I always try to use the variety called Spookie. These plants yield large numbers of fruit and ripen earlier than the larger varieties.

When Alexis was young, we used to take bushels of these small pumpkins to school for easy, manageable jack-o'-lanterns. We hoped they were used in pies once Halloween had passed.

I fashioned maple and dogwood leaves from leftover pâte brisée and puff pastry for this simple sugar pumpkin molasses pie. Baked separately, the leaves were placed on top just before serving.

T H E R E C I P E

Makes one 11-inch pie

ONE UNBAKED 11-INCH PÂTE BRISÉE PIE SHELL (PAGE 198), CHILLED

- **1 SUGAR PUMPKIN (APPROXIMATELY 3 POUNDS)**
- **4 EGGS, LIGHTLY BEATEN**
- **½ CUP HONEY**
- **¼ CUP MOLASSES**
- **½ CUP MILK**
- **½ CUP HEAVY CREAM**
- **½ TEASPOON GROUND GINGER**
- **½ TEASPOON CINNAMON**
- **1 TEASPOON SALT**

GARNISH: PASTRY LEAVES (PAGE 140), BAKED AND COOLED

1. Cut the pumpkin into large chunks, removing the seeds. Steam over boiling water in a heavy saucepan for 25 to 30 minutes, until fork-tender. Drain and let the pumpkin cool slightly. Using a sharp spoon, scrape the cooked pumpkin from the skin and put it in the bowl of a food processor. Purée until smooth.

2. Preheat the oven to 375°.

3. Measure out 3 cups of the puréed pumpkin, put it in a mixing bowl with the remaining ingredients, and stir thoroughly. Pour into the pie crust and bake for approximately 1 hour, until the filling is firm and the top a glossy brown. Let cool before serving. Garnish with pastry leaves.

CHAPTER 8.

WHEN I WAS A CHILD GROWING UP IN New Jersey, my family baked a lot with nuts. We purchased nuts in the shell from local markets or picked them from the ground at the end of the summer. We had all kinds of nuts—walnuts, filberts, almonds, Brazil nuts, and pecans—stored in baskets and bowls in dark, cool places. A collection of unusual but efficient nutcrackers was kept in the cupboard. Each of the nutcrackers had a specific purpose. There was an especially large, complex tool for cracking pecans without breaking the nutmeats, and even a special hammer for the black walnuts we gathered every autumn for cookies and ice cream. Nuts were our family's snack food, and every game of Scrabble or gin rummy was accompanied by the sound of cracking shells.

Nowadays, nuts of every variety are available shelled and even blanched and peeled. Nuts can be bought in perfect halves—pecans and walnuts for pie toppings—in less expensive pieces for use in fillings, and sliced, slivered, or ground. Nuts remain fresher, by the way, if kept in the freezer.

Because nuts have a strong and often somewhat bitter taste, most pie and tart fillings made with nuts are sweet and sticky. I like to temper this sweetness with additional flavors. I add orange peel to macadamia nut filling, for instance, lemon rind to a pecan tart, and liqueur and lemon zest to an almond tart. Semisweet chocolate is excellent in combination with nuts, too.

Nuts

Walnut Tartlets with Chocolate Lace

This delicate-looking yet rich walnut tartlet is served on an amethyst cut-glass plate. The table is covered with a nineteenth-century fruit-and-flowers chintz cloth.

You can serve desserts like this one in various sizes: in a tiny 2-inch tartlet size as an accompaniment to sorbet or ice cream, or in a 3½- to 4-inch size as the only dessert. The larger size makes an ample portion for one when the filling is very rich, as these walnut tartlets are.

These tartlets were baked and then decorated with a lacy chocolate filigree design and chocolate-dipped walnut halves. A handy hint if you don't have a pastry bag and metal tip: Spoon the melted chocolate into a small plastic bag and with a needle pierce a small hole in one corner. Gently squeeze the chocolate through the hole to create any design you wish.

THE RECIPE

Makes twelve 3½-inch tartlets

TWELVE 3½-INCH PÂTE BRISÉE TARTLET SHELLS (PAGE 198), PARTIALLY BAKED AND COOLED

- **2 EGGS, LIGHTLY BEATEN**
- **⅓ CUP GRANULATED SUGAR**
- **2 TEASPOONS GRAND MARNIER OR KIRSCH**
- **3 TABLESPOONS UNSALTED BUTTER, MELTED AND COOLED**
- **3 TABLESPOONS HEAVY CREAM**
- **¾ CUP LIGHT CORN SYRUP**
- **2 CUPS COARSELY CHOPPED WALNUTS**
- **6 OUNCES SEMISWEET CHOCOLATE, MELTED**

GARNISH: 12 WALNUT HALVES, COATED WITH A SMALL AMOUNT OF ADDITIONAL MELTED CHOCOLATE

1. Preheat the oven to 350°.

2. To make the filling, whisk the eggs and sugar together in a mixing bowl. Stir in the Grand Marnier, butter, cream, corn syrup, and chopped walnuts, mixing well. Spoon the mixture into the tartlet shells, dividing it evenly among them, and bake for approximately 30 minutes, until the filling is set. Remove to a wire rack and let the tartlets cool completely.

3. Stir the melted chocolate until smooth, and put it in a pastry bag fitted with a #0 tip. Pipe the chocolate onto the tops of the tartlets, zigzagging back and forth to create a lacy pattern. Garnish the center of each with a chocolate-dipped walnut half. Serve at room temperature.

On a recent vacation to Hawaii, I had the opportunity to see the large, round, dark-leaved macadamia trees, on which thousands of small, very hard-shelled nuts grow. I had always wondered how they grew, and how so small a state could produce enough for the world's consumption. I visited a nut factory and watched as the nuts were roasted, shelled, and packaged. I tasted raw nuts, salted nuts, nut brittle, syrup, and butter, but I still like the nuts plain-roasted best.

This recipe is one I discovered on my trip to the Pacific and adapted for this book. The filling for the plain pâte brisée tartlets is buttery, sweet, and crunchy. Candied orange peel, chopped for the filling and also used in the shape of bows for decorative garnish, gives the tartlets another layer of flavor.

My sister-in-law Rita Christiansen found these unusual plates at the Women's Exchange in Southport. The Art Nouveau-looking design has been painted onto fine white Royal Doulton china.

Macadamia Nut Tartlets

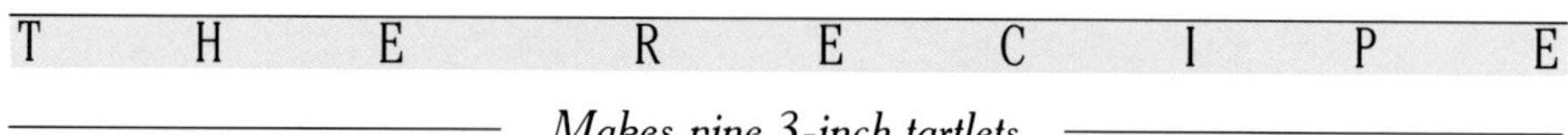

T H E R E C I P E

Makes nine 3-inch tartlets

NINE 3-INCH PÂTE BRISÉE TARTLET SHELLS (PAGE 198), PARTIALLY BAKED AND COOLED

¾ CUP CHOPPED UNSALTED MACADAMIA NUTS

CANDIED ORANGE PEEL (PAGE 101) FROM 1 LARGE BRIGHT-SKINNED ORANGE

11 TABLESPOONS (1⅜ STICKS) UNSALTED BUTTER

⅓ CUP GRANULATED SUGAR

3 TABLESPOONS HEAVY CREAM

1. Preheat the oven to 350°.

2. Using a very sharp knife or cleaver, coarsely chop the macadamia nuts and set aside. Finely chop half the candied orange peel and set aside. (Reserve the remaining candied orange peel for garnish.)

3. Melt the butter and sugar together in a heavy saucepan over medium heat, and then bring the mixture to a boil. Add the nuts, chopped orange peel, and cream. As soon as the mixture comes to a boil, take it off the heat.

4. Spoon the filling into the tartlet shells. Bake for approximately 20 minutes, until the filling is golden brown and caramelized. Let the tartlets cool on a wire rack. Garnish with the remaining candied orange peel, arranged in bows atop the tartlets.

8

NUTS

The almond tart is served on one of the opalescent hobnail plates I found at the Stock Market, a consignment shop in Westport. The old chintz coverlet is from this shop, too.

A slice of almond tart and a cup of lemon tea—a perfect afternoon sweet before a nap or while reading a favorite novel.

Almonds are very versatile, mild-flavored nuts that require simple ingredients—a small amount of Grand Marnier or kirsch and lemon or orange zest, for instance—to enhance their flavor. This tart is baked in a narrow, rectangular tart shell, but it could be baked in any shape pan or even as individual small tartlets. Remember to bake it on a parchment-covered baking sheet, though, because of the tendency of the filling to bubble over during baking.

Almond Tart

THE RECIPE

Makes one 4½ × 14-inch rectangular tart

ONE 4½ × 14-INCH PÂTE BRISÉE TART SHELL (PAGE 198), PARTIALLY BAKED AND COOLED

1½ CUPS SLICED BLANCHED ALMONDS
1½ CUPS HEAVY CREAM
1¼ CUPS GRANULATED SUGAR
PINCH OF SALT
2 TABLESPOONS GRAND MARNIER OR KIRSCH
⅛ TEASPOON ALMOND EXTRACT
ZEST OF 1 LEMON OR ORANGE

1. Preheat the oven to 350°.

2. Combine the almonds, cream, sugar, salt, Grand Marnier, and almond extract in a heavy saucepan and stir. Cook over low heat, stirring constantly, for 10 to 15 minutes, until the sugar dissolves. Remove from the heat and stir in the lemon zest. Pour the mixture into the prepared tart shell and bake for approximately 30 minutes, until the filling is set and caramel-colored. Let the tart cool slightly before removing it from the pan, but do not let the caramelized sugar harden completely or it will be very difficult to remove.

Ginger Wallace's Pecan Tart

This rectangular pecan tart, flavored with grated lemon rind, is served on a Scottish shortbread board dating from the eighteenth century.

Nut pies and tarts are usually rich and very sweet, often too much so, I think. For this reason, I decided to try this recipe from a friend in Tennessee for a pecan tart with a thinner filling, flavored with grated lemon rind. The traditional ingredients—corn syrup, molasses, brown sugar, eggs, and pecans—are still there, but in a somewhat unusual form.

We baked the tart in a pâte brisée crust that was made in a rectangular removable-bottom tart pan. Perfect pecan halves were used so that the patterned top would look very neat. Some people prefer very small pecans, but in any event, try to use unbroken halves.

T H E R E C I P E

Makes one 7½ × 11-inch rectangular tart

ONE UNBAKED 7½ × 11-INCH PÂTE BRISÉE TART SHELL (PAGE 198), WELL CHILLED

- 4 EGGS
- 1 CUP PACKED DARK BROWN SUGAR
- ¼ TEASPOON SALT
- ¼ CUP MOLASSES
- ¼ CUP LIGHT CORN SYRUP
- 3 TABLESPOONS UNSALTED BUTTER, MELTED AND COOLED
- 1 TEASPOON VANILLA EXTRACT
- GRATED RIND OF 1 LEMON OR ORANGE
- 1½ CUPS CHOPPED PECANS
- 1¼ CUPS PERFECT PECAN HALVES

1. Preheat the oven to 325°.

2. Put the eggs in a mixing bowl and beat with a fork. Blend in the sugar, salt, molasses, and corn syrup. Stir in the butter, vanilla, and lemon or orange rind, mixing until thoroughly blended. Add the chopped pecans.

3. Pour the filling mixture into the pastry shell and neatly arrange the pecan halves in rows on top. Bake for 45 to 50 minutes, until the pastry is lightly browned and the filling set. Let the tart cool on a rack before cutting and serving.

CHAPTER

WE HAVE ONE CLIENT WITH A SEEMingly insatiable appetite for chocolate desserts. Because we cater for her on a regular basis, we are always inventing or reinventing desserts of dark or white chocolate to serve at her dinner-soirees. The basic requirements are always the same—rich, dense, sinfully delicious, beautiful, and preferably easily served. This last request has meant that the tarts are made small, or that large tarts are cut in the kitchen and arranged on dessert plates before serving, so that each is decorative and individually perfect.

Chocolate is fun to work with, but only under certain conditions. The chocolate must be of very good quality, the temperature of the room cool, the air not too humid, and the work surface smooth (marble, steel, and slate are good). You also need good equipment—sturdy steel baking sheets (unscratched) and strong, straight scrapers for forming chocolate curls, thatch, and bark; and soft brushes for making chocolate leaves—as well as patience in a large degree.

I will never forget the class I taught in Florida. It was an unbearably hot, humid day, and the air conditioning malfunctioned halfway through the class. As if that weren't enough, the baking sheets I was using to make chocolate curls were scratched and the pastry scraper had a small dent in the edge. Although I had put the sheets of chocolate in the freezer, they softened almost immediately when I removed them to the demonstration counter. Patient chilling and quick scraping did finally manage to produce rather small but passable curls. When I looked up in relief, I saw smiling approvingly at me from the rear of the classroom a familiar, friendly face. It was the doyenne of chocolate curls, Maida Heatter, who had just dropped in to ask me to lunch!

Included in this chapter are several cream pies and custard tarts, which, like the chocolate tarts, require a bit more preparation than most of the other creations in this book. But they are favorites in my family, and are certainly worth the bit of additional effort.

Chocolate, Custards & Creams

This tart with its unusual chocolate "curls" tasted just as good as it should have—it only looked a bit different.

As mentioned before, working with chocolate is sometimes frustrating. When making the curls for this tart I experienced difficulty in getting the large free-form curls that I wanted for the top. Mine wanted to be small, tight spirals or large sheets. Still, I persevered, and saved all my unusual forms.

I baked a deep 8½-inch tart shell, using a plain pâte brisée. The chocolate mousse was made and the shell filled. Just before serving, I arranged the "curls" on top of the mousse. The tart looked asymmetrical, stark, and architectural, which I rather liked.

Several factors contributed to my failure to make the type of curls pictured on page 159. I had only small baking sheets on which to spread the melted chocolate; the pastry scraper to which I was accustomed had been borrowed and I was left with a smaller, thinner one; the chocolate got too cold, and I did not wait long enough for it to soften before making the curls.

Practice and patience generally make the forming of curls easier, but don't despair if they aren't perfect. The result, as here, can be equally delicious, and even more extraordinary to look at.

Chocolate Mousse "Architecture" Tart

THE RECIPE

Makes one deep 8½-inch tart

ONE DEEP 8½-INCH PÂTE BRISÉE TART SHELL (PAGE 198), BAKED AND COOLED

12 OUNCES SEMISWEET CHOCOLATE, CHOPPED
¼ CUP WATER
5 EGG YOLKS, LIGHTLY BEATEN
7 EGG WHITES
PINCH OF SALT

GARNISH: CHOCOLATE CURLS (PAGE 158)

1. Melt the chocolate with the water in the top of a double boiler, or in a low (200°) oven. When melted, remove from heat, add the egg yolks, and stir until smooth. Let the mixture cool almost completely.

2. Beat the egg whites with the salt until stiff, and quickly but gently fold them into the chocolate mixture. Spoon the mousse into the baked tart shell and refrigerate for at least 3 hours.

3. Garnish as desired with chocolate curls. Keep chilled until ready to serve.

Chocolate Curls, Bark & Thatch

1. Melt finely broken chocolate (semisweet, sweet, or white chocolate) in a glass or stainless steel bowl placed in a very low oven (200° for dark chocolate, 95° for white chocolate). Dark chocolate can also be melted in a double boiler over barely simmering water.* When melted, stir until smooth. Using a pastry scraper or a large spatula, spread the chocolate evenly on a sturdy flat baking sheet. (I use heavy-duty aluminum or stainless steel sheets with no or very low edges. Very large curls must be made on large sheets.) The chocolate should be spread as thinly as possible while remaining opaque on the baking sheet; if applied too thickly, it will not curl at all. Refrigerate or freeze until hardened.

2. Remove the baking sheet from the refrigerator. Using a sharp, metal pastry scraper, held at a 45° angle, scrape off a strip of chocolate from the pan; the chocolate will curl as it is scraped. Repeat until as much chocolate has been removed as possible. Chill or freeze the curls until firm and ready to use.

3. The type of curl you get will be determined largely by the temperature of the chocolate when you remove it from the refrigerator. If it is very cold, the chocolate will splinter when scraped and give you small "thatch." If the chocolate is a little less cold, you will produce tight curls. And if the chilled chocolate approaches room temperature (or if a lightly pressed finger leaves a slight print), you will have big, loose curls or sheets of chocolate, which can be used as "bark." The type of curl you produce will also depend on how you scrape the chocolate from the sheet. Just remember that making beautiful, perfect curls takes practice.

*NOTE: If the chocolate becomes too hot, it will turn lumpy and cloudy. Adding a teaspoon of vegetable shortening or clarified butter may smooth it out.

At right: *Dark and white chocolate curls, and "marbled" curls I made by drizzling white and dark chocolate on the baking sheet, smoothing with a pastry scraper, and proceeding as for the other curls.*

The chocolate is spread as evenly as possible using a pastry scraper.

Scraping white chocolate from the baking sheet.

9

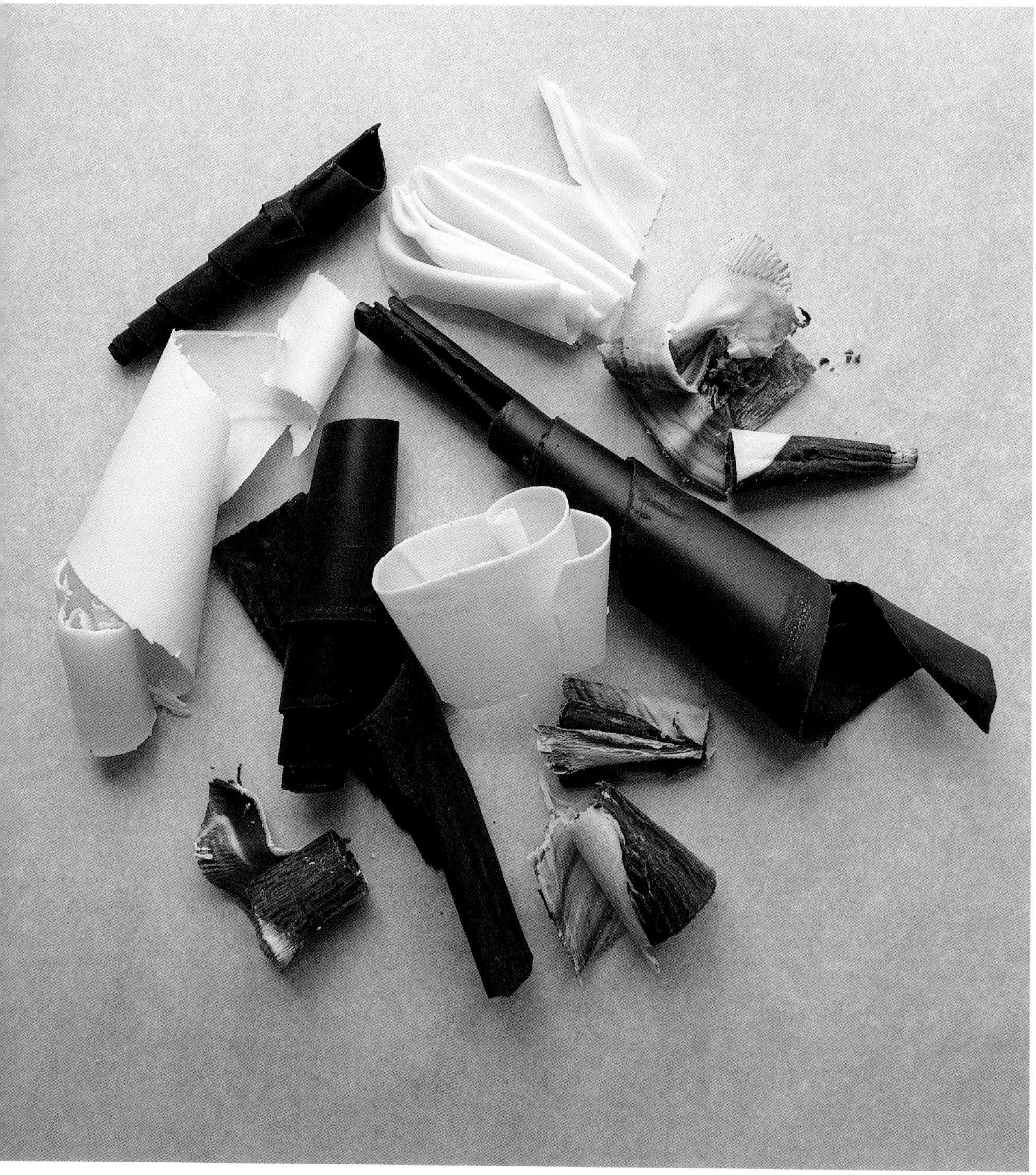

CHOCOLATE, CUSTARDS & CREAMS

Every Valentine's Day we cater a very special party at Susan and Tony Victoria's house in New York City. Guests are always invited for "heart-y" hors d'oeuvres and desserts, and it is my challenge each year to devise an unusual menu to fit the theme. Almost all the food, savory and sweet, is made in the shape of hearts. One exception this year was a huge "bouquet" of these edible white carnation tartlets, mixed in with real flowers: dark red carnations, red and pink roses, and white freesias. The bouquet was laid flat on the dessert buffet and tied lavishly with satin ribbons. Guests were surprised by the *trompe l'oeil* effect, and even more intrigued when they tasted the delicious white chocolate–mocha combination.

My friend Mariana Pasternak, a Romanian émigrée, gave me the idea for the wonderful combination of white chocolate with mocha. She pointed out that because white chocolate is so sweet, it needs to be counterbalanced by another flavor, her favorite being mocha or strong coffee. I folded instant espresso coffee into stiffly whipped cream for this tart filling. Small, jagged white chocolate curls, which looked very much like carnation petals, were inserted at random into the cream. The result: a very flowerlike creation.

White Chocolate-Mocha Cream Carnation Tartlets

T H E R E C I P E

Makes ten deep 3½-inch tartlets

TEN DEEP 3½-INCH PÂTE BRISÉE TARTLET SHELLS (PAGE 198), BAKED AND COOLED (WE USED SMALL BRIOCHE PANS)

1 CUP HEAVY CREAM
2 TEASPOONS INSTANT ESPRESSO POWDER
2 TABLESPOONS CONFECTIONERS' SUGAR

GARNISH: WHITE CHOCOLATE CURLS (PAGE 158)

1. Using a wire whisk or electric mixer, whip the cream until it has thickened. Gradually beat in the espresso powder and confectioners' sugar, and whip to stiff peaks. Be careful not to overbeat, or the cream will begin to turn to butter. (This can happen quickly if you are using an electric mixer.)

2. Divide the whipped cream evenly among the tartlet shells, and complete the tartlets by standing short curls of white chocolate in the whipped cream, arranging them to resemble carnation petals. Chill until serving time, up to 3 hours.

Above: *Two carnation tartlets sit on a pretty green octagonal Depression glass plate garnished with a piece of fresh heather.*

At right: *White carnation tartlets are served from a Japanese rice basket decorated with white roses and freesias.*

Chocolate Victoria Tartlets

I have been making chocolate Victoria tartlets for years. The filling for these bite-size, delectable desserts is simply a combination of very good chocolate—I like to use Callebaut, Lindt, Tobler, or Maillards—sugar, and heavy cream. The ingredients are warmed slowly until they become velvety smooth; then the filling is spooned carefully into paper-thin tartlet shells, and the tartlets are refrigerated. The chocolate mixture thickens well in the cold, yet retains a satiny gloss and texture.

Just before serving, I like to decorate the chocolate with whipped cream, which I pipe on with different tips. I sometimes garnish the tartlets with candied lilacs or violets, too. Their deep lavender color is unusually attractive against the glistening chocolate.

I use a simple pâte brisée for the tartlet shells, taking extreme care when rolling out the pastry to do a small amount at a time and to roll it very thin. If the consistency is correct (and this comes with practice), the resulting tartlet shells will be very thin, very tender, and yet sturdy enough to hold the filling without crumbling or chipping.

I make many different shapes and sizes of tartlets — some one-bite, some two- or three-bite-size. They can be served as finger desserts or as a fork-and-plate dessert.

THE RECIPE

Makes twelve 4-inch tartlets

TWELVE 4-INCH PÂTE BRISÉE TARTLET SHELLS (PAGE 198), BAKED AND COOLED

8 OUNCES SEMISWEET CHOCOLATE, CHOPPED

⅓ CUP GRANULATED SUGAR

2 CUPS HEAVY CREAM

GARNISH: WHIPPED CREAM
CANDIED VIOLETS OR LILACS (OPTIONAL)

1. To make the filling, melt the chocolate and sugar in a bain-marie, stirring constantly until very smooth. Add the cream and continue stirring for 8 to 10 minutes, until the mixture thickens. Let the mixture become completely cool but not set before filling the tartlet shells. Refrigerate the filled shells for at least 4 hours until set, overnight if possible.
2. Decorate with whipped cream piped through a pastry tip (we used an Ateco #2 round tip and a #67 leaf tip), and garnish with candied violets or lilacs, if desired. Chill until ready to serve, but no more than 2 hours, or the whipped cream will become watery.

At left: *We photographed these dainty tartlets in a sunlit corner of our porch on an old wicker desk. The gallery of the desk is filled with white narcissus, carnations, iris, snapdragons, and English ivy. I found the white opaline glass plates at a local tag sale years ago.*

Black-Bottom Tart

My mother and I have been making this tart, which was my father's favorite, for many years. It is an old-fashioned cream pie with whipped cream and chocolate. When we made it, we used a round pie shell, the whipped cream was put on with a spatula, and the chocolate was simply grated over the top. Now I make it in a variety of shapes, my favorite being the heart, with the whipped cream piped atop the custard and the chocolate fashioned into thatch—a variation on chocolate curls.

Not long ago I gave a dinner party to honor Joe Allen, the great American astronaut, and his wife, Bonnie. I served black-bottom tart to the fourteen guests, among them chef Roger Vergé, who pointed out that the tart was basically a bavarois with rum and chocolate. My mother and I, not being French, had never considered this homey pie a classic French dessert.

This tart is made in three stages. First, the tart shell is lined with dark chocolate custard (above left). *Then a rum-laced custard is spooned over the chocolate* (above right). *Finally, whipped cream is piped with a rose petal tip over the entire surface. Chocolate thatch garnishes the finished tart* (opposite).

T H E R E C I P E

Makes one 9-inch heart-shaped tart

ONE 9-INCH HEART-SHAPED PÂTE BRISÉE TART SHELL (PAGE 198), BAKED AND COOLED

- ¾ CUP GRANULATED SUGAR
- 4 TEASPOONS CORNSTARCH
- ½ CUP COLD MILK
- 1½ CUPS SCALDED MILK
- 4 EGGS, SEPARATED
- 1½ OUNCES SEMISWEET CHOCOLATE, MELTED
- 2 TEASPOONS VANILLA EXTRACT
- 1 ENVELOPE GELATIN
- ¼ CUP COLD WATER
- 1 TABLESPOON DARK RUM
- ¼ TEASPOON SALT
- ¼ TEASPOON CREAM OF TARTAR
- 1 CUP HEAVY CREAM

GARNISH: CHOCOLATE THATCH (PAGE 158)

1. In a heavy saucepan, dissolve ½ cup sugar and the cornstarch in the cold milk. Stir in the scalded milk, place the mixture over direct heat, and boil for 3 minutes, stirring constantly. Transfer the mixture to the top of a double boiler.

2. Beat the egg yolks in a small bowl and stir in 3 tablespoons of the milk mixture. (This will keep the egg yolks from curdling when added to the remaining hot milk.) Pour this back into the remaining milk mixture, and cook over simmering water for 3 to 4 minutes, stirring constantly, until the mixture becomes quite thick. Remove from the heat and put 1 cup of the custard in a small bowl. Stir in the melted chocolate and vanilla, and set aside to cool completely. When cooled, spread evenly in the tart shell and chill.

3. Meanwhile, soften the gelatin in the cold water and add to the remaining hot custard. (The gelatin will not dissolve properly if the custard has cooled.) Fold in the rum and let the mixture cool until it just begins to set.

4. Beat the egg whites with the salt and cream of tartar until stiff but not dry. Gradually beat in the remaining sugar, then fold the egg whites into the custard mixture. Spoon this evenly over the chocolate mixture. Chill until set.

5. Whip the cream until stiff and spread or pipe (we used an Ateco #122 rose petal tip) over the custard. Garnish as desired with chocolate thatch. Chill until ready to serve.

Fudge Tart with Crème Anglaise & Orange Sauce

THE RECIPE

Makes one deep 8-inch tart

ONE DEEP 8-INCH PÂTE BRISÉE TART SHELL (PAGE 198), BAKED AND COOLED

5 OUNCES SEMISWEET CHOCOLATE, FINELY CHOPPED
¾ CUP (1½ STICKS) UNSALTED BUTTER, CUT INTO SMALL PIECES
1½ CUPS GRANULATED SUGAR
⅔ CUP ALL-PURPOSE FLOUR
6 EGGS, LIGHTLY BEATEN

Crème Anglaise

Makes approximately 3 cups

2½ CUPS MILK
1 VANILLA BEAN
¾ CUP GRANULATED SUGAR
6 EGG YOLKS
2 TEASPOONS CORNSTARCH
2 TABLESPOONS COGNAC

Orange Sauce

Makes approximately ½ cup

¾ CUP FRESHLY SQUEEZED ORANGE JUICE
2 TABLESPOONS GRAND MARNIER
1 CUP GRANULATED SUGAR
1 TABLESPOON GRATED ORANGE RIND

1. Preheat the oven to 350°.

2. To make the filling, melt the chocolate and butter together in a bain-marie over simmering water. When melted, remove from the heat and stir to combine. Set aside to cool.

3. Combine the sugar, flour, and eggs in a mixing bowl and whisk until well blended. Stir in the chocolate-butter mixture. Pour the filling into the tart shell, and bake for approximately 1¼ hours, until the filling is set. Remove to a rack and let cool completely.

4. To make the crème anglaise, boil the milk and the vanilla bean for a minute or two. Remove the vanilla bean. Using an electric mixer, beat the sugar and egg yolks together until thick and fluffy. Add the cornstarch. Mixing on low speed, add the boiled milk, a little at a time. When thoroughly blended, transfer the mixture to a heavy enameled saucepan. Cook over low heat, stirring constantly, until the sauce thickens to a light, creamy mixture. (Do not let the mixture boil, however, or the egg yolks will curdle.) Remove the mixture from the heat and whisk in the Cognac. Strain the mixture through a fine sieve and let cool. Refrigerate until ready to use.

5. To make the orange sauce, combine the orange juice, Grand Marnier, and sugar in a heavy saucepan and cook over low heat, stirring constantly, until thick and syrupy and reduced by half. Remove from the heat, stir in the grated orange rind, and let cool.

6. To serve, place a piece of the tart on a plate and spoon crème anglaise around the bottom. Drizzle a small amount of orange sauce into the crème anglaise in swirls.

This chocolate fudge tart is a very dense, moist concoction that should please all true chocolate lovers. For the photograph I baked the filling in a deep (1½-inch) tart shell. Because there was so much filling, the tart took more than an hour to bake. The center of the tart was still very soft, but the perimeter was well set, and the top became crusty.

The two sauces, a thin crème anglaise and a thicker orange sauce, were served with the tart. For an unusual presentation, I first spooned the custard sauce on the dessert plates around a wedge of tart, then drizzled thin ribbons of the orange sauce into the crème anglaise.

At left: *Orange sauce swirls in the crème anglaise spooned around this rich, opulent-looking dessert.*

Two-Chocolate "Endpaper" Tart

When you open an old leather-bound book, you often find beautifully marbled handmade endpapers. This tart, a combination of chocolate Victoria filling and swirls of white chocolate Victoria, is easy to make and looks strikingly similar to those lovely endpapers.

White chocolate is difficult to work with and can be cloyingly sweet, to my taste. I find that it is best used sparingly and decoratively, as in this recipe, or as white chocolate curls or leaves.

I discovered the best way to melt white chocolate by accident. It was very hot in our baking room one day, and a half pound of white chocolate had inadvertently been left out near the oven. It had become completely soft in its brown paper wrapping; scooped out of the package, the chocolate was perfectly melted and smooth. Now when I melt white chocolate, I break it into small pieces, place them in a glass or stainless steel bowl, cover with plastic wrap to keep it from drying out, and put it in a very warm spot (90° to 95°), but not in a hot oven or over simmering water. The white chocolate softens perfectly this way and never becomes grainy or oily.

Chocolate leaves, made from ivy, galax, and lemon leaves, surround this tart as edible garnishes. It is served on a highly polished rosewood tray.

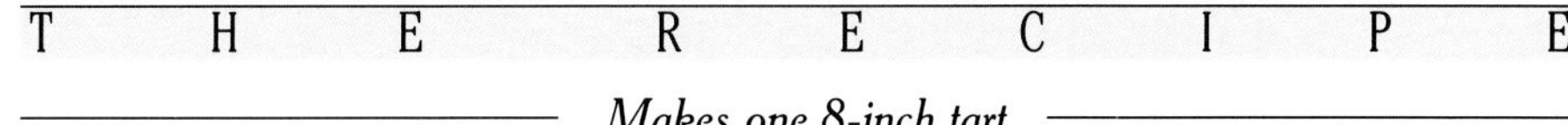

THE RECIPE

Makes one 8-inch tart

ONE 8-INCH PÂTE BRISÉE TART SHELL (PAGE 198), BAKED AND COOLED

4 OUNCES WHITE CHOCOLATE
3 TABLESPOONS HEAVY CREAM

CHOCOLATE VICTORIA FILLING (PAGE 163)

GARNISH: CHOCOLATE LEAVES (PAGE 171)

1. To melt the white chocolate, break it into small pieces, put it in a glass or stainless steel bowl, cover with plastic wrap, and place in a very warm place (a 95° oven is ideal) until soft. Stir the chocolate until smooth, add the cream, and mix well. Set aside.

2. Pour the chocolate Victoria filling into the baked tart shell. Dribble the melted white chocolate over the filling and, using a sharp knife, draw it through to blend the white chocolate into the dark, creating a marbled effect. Refrigerate the tart until the filling is set, overnight if possible. Garnish with chocolate leaves, if desired.

Chocolate Leaves

Opposite page: *White and dark chocolate broken up into bits before melting.*

Left: *Leaves are coated with melted chocolate using a small pastry brush.*

1. Put finely broken chocolate (semisweet, sweet, or white chocolate) in a glass or stainless steel bowl, and set in a low oven (200° for dark chocolate, 95° for white chocolate). Dark chocolate can also be melted in a double boiler over barely simmering water. Stir the melted chocolate until smooth. The chocolate must be thin enough to spread evenly and smoothly.

2. Choose perfect leaves from trees and shrubs, or purchase them from a florist. (Shown here are lemon, galax, and ivy leaves; I also like holly, maple, and beech.) Strong leaves with a leathery texture will hold up better than very delicate leaves. Using a small, fine ½-inch pastry brush, apply the chocolate to the shiny side of the leaf. Work quickly, with as few brushstrokes as possible. Cover the entire leaf but do not let any chocolate dribble onto the underside of the leaf; the chocolate will not pull away in one piece if the edge is not perfectly clean. Dark chocolate should require only one coat; the thinner white chocolate will need two or three applications. Just be sure to chill the leaves between coats until the chocolate is completely hardened. Carefully place the chocolate-covered leaves on a parchment-lined baking sheet, and freeze or refrigerate until the chocolate is completely hardened.

3. Gently peel the leaf away from the chocolate. This requires speed and extreme delicacy. The larger the leaf, the more difficult it is to prevent breakage. After you peel away a chocolate leaf, immediately refrigerate it on a parchment-covered baking sheet. I find it best to work right next to the refrigerator and keep all the leaves except the one I'm working on in the cold. Store chocolate leaves in the freezer indefinitely for future use.

Chocolate Pecan Lattice Tart

Wonderful things can be created with ordinary pâte brisée. Complicated-looking crusts decorated with pastry leaves, braids, fancy crimped edges, and elaborate lattices are fun to make, even if they are more time-consuming than simple bottom-crust pies. Once the basic pâte brisée recipe is mastered, all you need is a floured board, a good rolling pin, a sharp knife, and a pastry wheel or two.

Chocolate pecan filling can be too sweet for some tastes. Covering this tart with a pastry lattice cuts down on the sweetness and makes this old favorite especially pretty to look at.

THE RECIPE

Makes one 11-inch double-crust tart

ONE UNBAKED 11-INCH PÂTE BRISÉE TART SHELL (PAGE 198), PLUS EXTRA PASTRY FOR THE LATTICE TOP, CHILLED

- **3 OUNCES SEMISWEET CHOCOLATE, CHOPPED**
- **3 TABLESPOONS UNSALTED BUTTER**
- **⅔ CUP GRANULATED SUGAR**
- **1 CUP LIGHT CORN SYRUP**
- **3 EGGS**
- **1 TEASPOON VANILLA EXTRACT**
- **1 CUP COARSELY CHOPPED PECANS**

GARNISH: CHOCOLATE LEAVES (PAGE 171)
PECAN HALVES

1. Melt the chocolate and butter together in the top of a double boiler, or in a glass or stainless steel bowl set in a low (200°) oven. Stir to combine and set aside.

2. In a medium-size heavy saucepan, combine the sugar and corn syrup and stir to partially dissolve the sugar. Bring this mixture to a boil, reduce the heat, and simmer for 2 minutes, stirring constantly with a wooden spoon. Remove from the heat.

3. Put the eggs in a mixing bowl and beat well with a fork. Stir in the chocolate-butter mixture. Whisk in the syrup and blend thoroughly. Stir in the vanilla and chopped pecans, and set the filling aside to cool completely.

4. Preheat the oven to 400°.

5. While the filling is cooling, make the lattice top. Roll out the pastry to a thickness of less than ⅛ inch and, using a pastry wheel, cut it into ½-inch strips. Working directly on a sheet of parchment paper, carefully weave the strips together as closely as possible; you should have a woven lattice top that measures at least 12 × 12 inches, with no holes or spaces. Place another piece of parchment on top, and chill until ready to use.

6. Pour the filling into the chilled pastry crust, distributing the nuts as evenly as possible. Remove the lattice top from the refrigerator and, keeping it between the sheets of parchment, fold it in half. Holding it in your hand, remove the outside sheet of parchment. Place it over half the pie and carefully unfold the lattice to cover the filling. Gently remove the top sheet of parchment. Using your thumbs, cut off the excess pastry crust and lattice.

7. Bake the tart for 20 minutes at 400°, then lower the heat to 350° and bake until the crust is evenly browned and the filling set, approximately 25 minutes longer. Serve at room temperature, garnished with chocolate leaves and pecan halves.

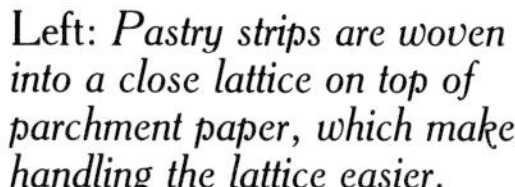

Left: *Pastry strips are woven into a close lattice on top of parchment paper, which makes handling the lattice easier.*

Below: *The baked tart, garnished with chocolate leaves and pecans, is served from an old Japanese rice basket.*

Crème Brûlée Tartlets

I used heart-shaped tin molds to make these tartlet shells filled with crème brûlée. The tarts are displayed on shelves in what once was a tall clock case.

Crème brûlée, a traditional dessert that is especially favored in the South, has had an extraordinary resurgence in popularity the last few years, due in large part to the inventiveness of California chefs. Flavored with fresh ginger, cardamom, and other spices, or with berries and fruits, taken out of fluted baking dishes and put in buttery tart shells, crème brûlée has become an exciting new dessert.

My favorite crème brûlée tart is served at Jams, one of New York's best restaurants; the recipe that follows is an adaptation of chef James Brinkley's recipe. It is wonderful with the fresh ginger, but I like it plain as well.

The topping for crème brûlée can be made with granulated white sugar or with brown sugar. I use a hand-held propane torch to melt the sugar, and find that I get a smoother, glassier top when I use white sugar. The propane torch has another good use—when cutting cakes and tarts, it is a good idea to run the blade of a sharp knife through the flame of the torch before each cut. A hot knife cuts right through the hard sugar topping or through a crumbly dacquoise.

T H E R E C I P E

Makes twelve shallow 3-inch tartlets

TWELVE 3-INCH PÂTE BRISÉE TARTLET SHELLS (PAGE 198), BAKED AND COOLED

- **2 CUPS HEAVY CREAM**
- **1 VANILLA BEAN**
- **4 EGG YOLKS, LIGHTLY BEATEN AND STRAINED**
- **¼ CUP GRANULATED SUGAR**
- **1½ TABLESPOONS COLD UNSALTED BUTTER, CUT INTO SMALL PIECES**
- **APPROXIMATELY ¼ CUP GRANULATED SUGAR FOR CARAMELIZING**

1. To make the crème brûlée, put the cream and the vanilla bean in a heavy saucepan and bring to a boil. Reduce the heat and simmer the mixture for 5 minutes, stirring occasionally. Set aside.

2. Combine the egg yolks and sugar and whisk together in a bain-marie over simmering water until pale and fluffy. The mixture should become dense but it must not scramble; be sure that the heat is not too high. Whisking constantly, strain the cream into the egg-sugar mixture. Continue cooking in the bain-marie for approximately 10 minutes, or until the mixture thickens and coats the back of a spoon. Take care not to overcook, or the mixture will separate. Remove from the heat and quickly whisk in the butter. Cover with plastic wrap and let cool to room temperature.

3. Spoon the custard evenly into the baked tartlet shells and refrigerate for at least 4 hours, until the crème brûlée is set.

4. Immediately before serving, sprinkle a small amount of granulated sugar on top of each custard tartlet and caramelize. I use a propane torch on low for this job. To avoid burning the crust, place thin strips of foil on the edges of the pastry. Remove the foil immediately after torching. You can also slide the tartlets under the broiler to caramelize the sugar.

VARIATIONS: This crème brûlée is so delicious and delicately flavored that it goes perfectly with many other ingredients. Pour the crème brûlée over thin slices of sautéed apples and refrigerate, or serve it with any type of fresh berry. Two tablespoons of candied orange peel (page 101) could also be stirred into the crème brûlée. Spices are also a wonderful accompaniment to its smooth taste; try ½ teaspoon freshly grated nutmeg or mace. Jams Restaurant in New York City makes a wonderful ginger crème brûlée by simmering 2 ounces peeled and ground fresh ginger with the heavy cream and vanilla bean.

I use a propane torch on low to caramelize the sugar sprinkled on top of these tartlets. The sugar hardens to a glassy coating this way.

The whipped cream on top of this luscious coconut tart is piped on with an Ateco #48 tip. It is served on an oval cherry Shaker tray.

This tart is made with an old-fashioned coconut cream pie filling. The whipped cream topping, which in more traditional recipes is mounded on top of the filling, is here carefully piped on top. I used freshly grated coconut in the filling, and fresh coconut curls for a decorative topping.

Fresh coconuts are available almost all year long. Choose whole coconuts that are heavy and full of liquid. Pierce one or two of the eyes with a corkscrew or ice pick and drain the coconut milk into a glass. Put the coconut on a baking sheet in a 350° oven and bake for about 12 to 15 minutes, until the shell cracks. Remove the coconut from the oven, crack open, and, with the point of a sharp knife, pry the white flesh from the shell. Peel the brown membrane from the white meat, grate the coconut for the filling, and using a vegetable peeler, make curls to use for the garnish.

Coconut Cream Tart

THE RECIPE

Makes one 11½-inch tart

ONE 11½-INCH PÂTE BRISÉE TART SHELL (PAGE 198), BAKED AND COOLED

- **1 CUP GRANULATED SUGAR**
- **½ CUP CORNSTARCH**
- **½ TEASPOON SALT**
- **4½ CUPS SCALDED MILK**
- **8 EGG YOLKS, LIGHTLY BEATEN**
- **2 TEASPOONS VANILLA EXTRACT**
- **2 CUPS FRESHLY GRATED COCONUT (OR FLAKED UNSWEETENED COCONUT)**
- **2 TABLESPOONS UNSALTED BUTTER**
- **1 CUP HEAVY CREAM**

GARNISH: FRESH COCONUT CURLS

1. In a heavy saucepan, combine the sugar, cornstarch, and salt. Stir in the scalded milk and mix until smooth. Cook over medium heat, stirring constantly, for 5 to 7 minutes, until the mixture thickens. Transfer the mixture to the top of a double boiler.

2. Whisk 4 tablespoons of the hot milk into the beaten egg yolks until well blended. Stir this mixture into the remaining hot milk and cook over simmering water until the custard is smooth and quite thick. Remove from heat and stir in the vanilla, coconut, and butter. Pour the custard into the baked tart shell and refrigerate until well set.

3. Whip the cream until stiff and pipe as desired over the cold custard (we used an Ateco #48 tip). Garnish with fresh coconut curls and chill until ready to serve.

NOTE: This recipe may be halved for a smaller (8- to 9-inch) tart.

There are few desserts as comforting as rice pudding. Whenever Andy and I are doing unpleasant tasks like taxes or cleaning the basement, I will make rice pudding or rice pudding tartlets to help us through. Served with a glass of milk or a pot of freshly brewed tea, these tartlets are hearty, satisfying, and delicious.

The rice pudding can be made in advance and spooned into tartlet shells, to be baked at the last minute. I added both currants and prunes to these tartlets. For variety, omit the prunes and add the grated rind of a lemon to the pudding.

Andy was doing a cash flow analysis for his publishing company one snowy Sunday afternoon, and photographer Beth Galton captured his paper-strewn table just as I served us rice pudding tartlets. The octagonal green-rimmed plates are old Wedgwood.

Rice Pudding Tartlets with Prunes & Currants

THE RECIPE

Makes six 4½-inch tartlets

SIX 4½-INCH PÂTE BRISÉE TARTLET SHELLS (PAGE 198), PARTIALLY BAKED AND COOLED

- **1 CUP LONG-GRAIN RICE**
- **1 CUP MILK**
- **2 WHOLE EGGS PLUS 2 EGG YOLKS, LIGHTLY BEATEN**
- **¼ CUP GRANULATED SUGAR**
- **¼ CUP DRIED CURRANTS**
- **1 CUP HEAVY CREAM**
- **PINCH OF SALT**
- **½ TEASPOON VANILLA EXTRACT**
- **1 TABLESPOON KIRSCH (OPTIONAL)**
- **3 PITTED PRUNES, HALVED**

1. Put the rice in a heavy saucepan, cover with water, and bring to a boil. Reduce the heat, cover, and continue to cook for approximately 20 minutes, until the rice is almost tender. Remove from the heat and drain.

2. Stir the milk into the rice and cook over low heat for approximately 20 to 25 minutes, until the mixture is thick and the rice is very tender. Remove from the heat.

3. Preheat the oven to 350°.

4. Add the remaining ingredients (except the prunes) to the rice-milk mixture and stir until well incorporated. Spoon the mixture into the partially baked tartlet shells (approximately ⅔ cup for each tartlet), and place a prune half in the center of each. Bake for approximately 30 minutes, until the filling is set and lightly golden. Serve warm or at room temperature.

Buttermilk pie is flaky, golden, and light as a feather.

When we plan a large Tex-Mex or Mexican party, with finger foods such as quesadillas, nachos, fajitas, corn cups with chili, grilled meats, seviche, etc., we often include buttermilk pie for dessert, accompanied by platters of fresh fruit. The filling is rich (note the sugar and butter), but it is also light, silken, and flavorful. The slightly sour taste of the buttermilk, heightened by the lemon juice, lemon zest, and nutmeg, cuts the richness of the other ingredients and offers guests a surprising, unusual custardlike pie.

We baked this buttermilk pie in a pâte brisée crust. The pan was an old hexagonal tin plate that I found at a tag sale years ago. The edges of this pie tin are quite wide and perfect for the application of the decorative leaf edging that we placed around the perimeter of the crust. (See page 204 for complete instructions.)

Something wonderful happens to the pastry when baked with this particular filling. It may have to do with the baking tin, but I think it has to do with the fact that the butter and milk in the filling make the crust even more tender and flaky than usual, and even more golden.

The leaf edging is applied with cold water and brushed with an egg yolk glaze.

T H E R E C I P E

Makes one 8½-inch pie

ONE UNBAKED 8½-INCH PÂTE BRISÉE PIE SHELL (PAGE 198), WELL CHILLED, PLUS PÂTE BRISÉE LEAVES FOR EDGE OF CRUST

GLAZE: 1 EGG YOLK BEATEN WITH 2 TEASPOONS WATER

- 1¼ CUPS GRANULATED SUGAR
- 3 TABLESPOONS ALL-PURPOSE FLOUR
- 4 EGGS, LIGHTLY BEATEN
- ½ CUP (1 STICK) UNSALTED BUTTER, MELTED AND COOLED SLIGHTLY
- 1 CUP BUTTERMILK
- ZEST OF 1 LEMON
- 1 TABLESPOON FRESHLY SQUEEZED LEMON JUICE
- 1 TEASPOON VANILLA EXTRACT
- FRESHLY GRATED NUTMEG TO TASTE

1. Preheat the oven to 425°.

2. Affix the pastry leaves around the edge of the pie crust with cold water. Brush the leaves with the egg yolk glaze. Refrigerate until ready to fill.

3. Combine the sugar and flour in a large mixing bowl. Add the beaten eggs and mix well. Stir in the butter and buttermilk. Stir in the lemon rind and juice, vanilla, and nutmeg, and pour into the pie shell. Place the pie in the center of the oven for 15 minutes. Lower the heat to 350° and continue to bake for approximately 40 minutes, until the filling is set. Remove from the oven and serve at room temperature.

CHAPTER 10.

ON A LOVELY AUTUMN DAY LAST year, I gave a pie party for my friends, neighbors, and family to celebrate the completion of the photographs for this book. The invitations read "B.Y.O.P." (Bring Your Own Pie). Everyone brought their favorite pies or tarts in appropriate carrying baskets, as well as large appetites. More than twenty-five desserts were assembled on a huge barn table. The weather was accommodating: warm sunlight and light breezes. Children ran or crawled, stopping now and then to taste a slice (or fistful) of pie. Pitchers of iced tea and a silver service for hot tea were set out on another wooden table in the garden.

Kathy Powell, who helped orchestrate the whole thing, eliminated duplications in the offerings by judicious phone calling and gentle persuasion. The array was delightful, varied, and colorful. We put a giant chintz coverlet on the table and its soft, aged tones made it a perfect background for all the pies and tarts. I made a few fruit and berry tarts, for fun, and of course my Mile-High Lemon Meringue Pie, by popular demand.

This wasn't a pie contest, but all the guests agreed that a few pies really were extra-special, and I have included the recipes for these. My sister-in-law Rita Christiansen's Raspberry-Rhubarb Lattice Pie was my personal favorite. This surprised me, because I don't like strawberry-rhubarb pie and had not even intended to include a recipe for one in the book. But Rita's raspberry-rhubarb combination tasted very different, and it wasn't at all mushy, the way strawberry pies can be.

A party of this nature, communal in offering and informal in plan, needs space, beverages, and lots of plates and forks and pie servers. Baskets of fresh fruit—apples, pears, or peaches—and bowls of berries are excellent if there are going to be lots of children. Small blankets or coverlets and pillows are great for sitting on the ground if there are not enough chairs and tables available..

The Pie Party

Guests:
Clockwise from top left: *Ellie Giannone with Michael and Katie, Laura Herbert and Sophie, Rita Christiansen and Kirk, Debbie Lonsdale and Bronwen, Marsha Harris, Donna Scott, Rosanna Jolis, Kathy Evans with Carter and Morgan, Kathy Powell*

Pies:
Top row (left to right): *Rita Christiansen's Raspberry-Rhubarb Pie,* Laura Herbert's Pecan Cheese Pie, Rosanna Jolis's Fig Tart with Pink Peppercorn Glaze,* Debbie Lonsdale's Apple Croustade, Kathy Evans's Kiwi-Persimmon Tart, Robyn Fairclough's Cranberry-Apple-Raisin Pie*

Middle row: *Marion Barnes's Mom's Apple Pie, Marinda Freeman's Great-Grandmother Middleton's Mincemeat Pie,* Martha's Strawberry Tart in Nut Crust, Martha's Mile-High Lemon Meringue Pie,* Dorian Leigh Parker's Blueberry Dumpling Pie, Taira Rappaport's Pyramid Pear Galette, Helen Evans's Blackberry-Apple Pie*

Bottom Row: *Laura's Chocolate Pecan Pie, Donna Scott's Sugar Pie,* Wendye Pardue's Cranberry-Raisin Pie,* Kathy Powell's Pear Tart with Chocolate Pastry Cream, Martha's Black Grape Tart in Nut Crust, Martha's Heart-Shaped Red Raspberry Tart, Marsha Harris's Lemon Pie,* Jody Thompson's Old-Fashioned Apple Pie*

*Recipes for these pies and tarts are given in this chapter.

Martha's Mile-High Lemon Meringue Pie

THE RECIPE

Makes one 9-inch pie

ONE 9-INCH PÂTE BRISÉE PIE SHELL (PAGE 198), BAKED AND COOLED

1¼ CUPS GRANULATED SUGAR
⅔ CUP SIFTED CAKE FLOUR
¼ CUP CORNSTARCH
PINCH OF SALT
1½ CUPS WATER
5 EGG YOLKS
½ CUP FRESHLY SQUEEZED LEMON JUICE
2 TABLESPOONS GRATED LEMON RIND
4 TABLESPOONS (½ STICK) UNSALTED BUTTER, CUT INTO SMALL PIECES

Meringue

8 TO 12 EGG WHITES
½ TEASPOON CREAM OF TARTAR
½ TEASPOON VANILLA EXTRACT
PINCH OF SALT
6 TABLESPOONS GRANULATED SUGAR

1. To make the filling, combine the sugar, flour, cornstarch, salt, and water in a bain-marie over simmering water, and cook for 10 to 20 minutes, until the mixture becomes very thick and almost translucent. Remove from the heat and beat in the egg yolks, one at a time, until thoroughly blended. Return to the heat and cook for 6 to 7 minutes, stirring constantly, until thick and smooth. Remove from the heat and stir in the lemon juice and rind. Whisk in the butter, a piece at a time, and set aside to cool.

2. Preheat the oven to 375°.

3. To make the meringue, beat the egg whites until fluffy. Add the cream of tartar, vanilla, and salt. Continue beating and add 1 tablespoon sugar to the mixture every minute. Beat for 7 to 8 minutes, until stiff peaks form.

4. Pour the cooled filling into the pie shell. Mound the meringue over the filling in peaks as high as possible, making sure to cover the filling completely to the edge of the pie shell.

5. Bake for approximately 10 minutes, or until the meringue is golden brown. Let cool at room temperature for at least 3 hours before cutting. Do not refrigerate.

NOTE: Cake flour is essential for the filling to thicken properly.

This pie, which has become a family favorite, originated one day when my mother and I had extra egg whites on hand. We made the meringue as high as the oven would allow!

THE PIE PARTY

Rita Christiansen's Raspberry-Rhubarb Lattice Pie

T H E   R E C I P E

Makes one 11-inch double-crust pie

PÂTE BRISÉE (PAGE 198) FOR AN 11-INCH DOUBLE-CRUST PIE, CHILLED

- **1½ TO 2 CUPS RASPBERRIES, FRESH OR FROZEN AND THAWED (UNSWEETENED ONLY)**
- **4 CUPS RHUBARB, FRESH OR FROZEN AND THAWED, CUT INTO 1-INCH PIECES**
- **1¼ CUPS GRANULATED SUGAR, OR TO TASTE**
- **⅓ CUP SIFTED ALL-PURPOSE FLOUR**
- **1 TEASPOON FRESHLY SQUEEZED LEMON JUICE**
- **1 TABLESPOON COLD UNSALTED BUTTER, CUT INTO SMALL PIECES**

GLAZE: 1 EGG BEATEN WITH 2 TABLESPOONS HEAVY CREAM

1. Preheat the oven to 350°.

2. Separate one-third of the pastry and refrigerate it, well wrapped, until ready to use. Roll out the remaining two-thirds for the bottom crust. Fit it into an 11-inch pie plate and chill.

3. Put the raspberries and rhubarb in a large mixing bowl and sprinkle with the sugar, flour, and lemon juice. Toss very gently, so as not to break the raspberries. Spoon the filling into the pie shell and dot with butter. Refrigerate while you prepare the lattice top.

4. Roll out the pastry for the lattice and cut it into ½-inch strips. Weave the strips together over the filling, and place an extra strip or two along the edge, where the bottom crust joins the lattice top; press this strip with the tines of a fork to seal well. Brush the lattice and all pastry edges with the glaze, and place the pie on a large parchment-covered baking sheet (to protect the oven from dripping fruit juices).

5. Bake for about 1½ hours, until the pastry is golden brown and the juices in the center of the pie are bubbling. Let cool on a rack before serving.

NOTE: If you use frozen fruit, be sure it is completely thawed and well drained.

Wendye Pardue's Cranberry-Raisin Pie

I don't especially like mixtures of fruits in pies, but Rita's combination of rhubarb and raspberry (back of basket) is sensational. In the front of the basket is Wendye's luscious cranberry-raisin pie.

T H E R E C I P E

Makes one 9-inch double-crust pie

TWO 11-INCH CIRCLES OF PÂTE BRISÉE (PAGE 198), CHILLED

2 CUPS FRESH CRANBERRIES
1½ CUPS GOLDEN RAISINS
½ CUP SUGAR, OR TO TASTE
¼ CUP MAPLE SYRUP
½ TEASPOON VANILLA EXTRACT
DASH OF BRANDY
GRATED RIND OF 1 ORANGE
2 TABLESPOONS COLD UNSALTED BUTTER, CUT INTO SMALL PIECES

1. Preheat the oven to 425°.

2. Press one round of pastry into a 9-inch pie plate. Chill. From the remaining pastry cut as many lattice strips as possible. Place the strips on a parchment-lined or water-sprayed baking sheet and chill.

3. Put the cranberries and raisins in a large mixing bowl. Sprinkle on the remaining ingredients except the butter and toss to combine, thoroughly coating the cranberries and raisins. Pour this mixture into the chilled bottom pastry and weave the strips over the filling to make the lattice. Trim and crimp the edges as desired.

4. Bake on a parchment-covered baking sheet for 15 minutes, reduce the heat to 350°, and continue to bake for approximately 35 to 40 minutes, until the crust is golden brown and the juices in the center of the pie bubble. Let cool before serving.

Marinda Freeman's Mincemeat Pie

THE RECIPE

Makes one 9-inch double-crust pie

TWO 9-INCH CIRCLES OF PÂTE BRISÉE (PAGE 198), CHILLED

½ QUART HOMEMADE MINCEMEAT (SEE BELOW)
2 CUPS TART APPLES, PEELED, CORED, AND CHOPPED
¼ TO ½ CUP GRANULATED SUGAR, TO TASTE

1. Preheat the oven to 450°. Press one of the pastry rounds into a 9-inch pie plate and chill.

2. Combine the mincemeat, apples, and sugar. Spoon the mixture into the pie shell, top with the remaining pastry round, and trim and crimp the edges as desired. Cut vent holes in the top crust to allow the steam to escape.

3. Bake for 30 minutes, until the crust is evenly browned. Let cool before serving.

Marinda used her great-grandmother Middleton's family recipe for this mincemeat filling. She brought the pie to the party in a large round wicker basket lined with a white linen cloth that had belonged to her great-grandmother.

Mincemeat

Makes 16 to 20 quarts

6 POUNDS SCRAGGY BEEF (NECK MEAT)
3 POUNDS SUET
4 POUNDS RAISINS
4 POUNDS CURRANTS
1 POUND CITRON, CHOPPED
2 POUNDS CANDIED FRUIT PEEL (GRAPEFRUIT, ORANGE, LEMON, PINEAPPLE PIECES), CHOPPED
12 POUNDS TART APPLES (SUCH AS JONATHAN), PEELED, CORED, AND CHOPPED
4½ OUNCES GROUND CINNAMON
1 OUNCE GROUND GINGER
1 OUNCE GROUND CLOVES
4 OUNCES FRESHLY GRATED NUTMEG
JUICE AND GRATED RIND OF 2 LEMONS
4 TABLESPOONS SALT
1 TEASPOON PEPPER
2 POUNDS GRANULATED SUGAR
1 QUART MOLASSES
1 QUART APPLE CIDER

1. Put the beef in a pot, cover with water, and simmer for 1½ to 2 hours, until tender. Reserve the liquid. Let the meat cool and remove any gristle. Chop the meat in a food processor or meat grinder until finely ground.

2. Cut the suet up into golf-ball-size pieces. Chill well. Chop fine by pulsing in batches in a food processor or by using a meat grinder.

3. Mix the beef and suet in a large bowl (or washtub) with all the remaining ingredients except the molasses and cider. Warm the liquid the beef was cooked in, and stir in the molasses and cider. Add to the mincemeat and mix well. Adjust spices to taste. Let cool.

4. Pack into plastic 1-quart containers and freeze. (Or, as was done before there were freezers, pack into 1-quart canning jars, pour a thin layer of molasses on top, and set in a cool place.) Mincemeat needs to age for about a month before use, so take the container out of the freezer a month ahead of time, pour a thin layer of molasses on top, put the cover back on, and refrigerate for a month.

Donna Scott's Sugar Pie

T H E R E C I P E

Makes one 9-inch pie

ONE 9-INCH PÂTE BRISÉE SHELL (PAGE 198), BAKED AND COOLED

- **¾ CUP PACKED BROWN SUGAR**
- **¼ CUP VANILLA SUGAR (PAGE 55), PLUS EXTRA FOR THE TOP**
- **⅓ CUP SIFTED ALL-PURPOSE FLOUR**
- **2 CUPS LIGHT CREAM**
- **1½ TEASPOONS VANILLA EXTRACT**
- **1 TEASPOON FRESHLY SQUEEZED LEMON JUICE**
- **1 TEASPOON BRANDY**
- **4 TABLESPOONS (½ STICK) COLD UNSALTED BUTTER, CUT INTO SMALL PIECES**
- **FRESHLY GRATED NUTMEG**

1. Preheat the oven to 350°.

2. Mix the sugars and flour together and sprinkle evenly over the bottom of the pie shell.

3. In a separate bowl, combine the cream, vanilla, lemon juice, and brandy. Pour this into the pie shell. Dot with butter and sprinkle with nutmeg.

4. Bake the pie for 40 to 45 minutes, until the filling is set. Let cool slightly, sprinkle with additional vanilla sugar, and serve.

Donna brought her delicious pie, liberally sprinkled with sugar, in a vine basket lined with a linen dishcloth.

Marsha Harris's Lemon Pie

This unusual chocolate cookie crust holds a wonderful sour lemon filling. Marsha topped the pie with whipped cream and decorated it with golden raspberries and mint leaves.

THE RECIPE

Makes one 9-inch pie

Chocolate Cookie Crust

- ½ CUP (1 STICK) UNSALTED BUTTER
- 8 OUNCES SEMISWEET CHOCOLATE, PLUS 2 TO 3 ADDITIONAL OUNCES, AS NECESSARY
- ½ CUP AMARETTI COOKIE CRUMBS
- 1 CUP FINE PLAIN WHITE BREAD CRUMBS, SLIGHTLY TOASTED
- ½ CUP FINELY GROUND ALMONDS
- 2 TABLESPOONS BROWN SUGAR

- 1 CUP GRANULATED SUGAR
- ½ CUP CORNSTARCH
- PINCH OF SALT
- ½ CUP FRESHLY SQUEEZED LEMON JUICE
- 1⅓ CUPS WATER
- 4 EGG YOLKS, LIGHTLY BEATEN
- 4 TABLESPOONS (½ STICK) UNSALTED BUTTER, CUT INTO SMALL PIECES, AT ROOM TEMPERATURE

GARNISH: SOFTLY WHIPPED CREAM

1. Preheat the oven to 325°.

2. To make the crust, melt the butter and chocolate together in the top of a double boiler. Set aside to cool slightly. Combine the cookie crumbs, bread crumbs, almonds, and brown sugar in the bowl of a food processor and process until well mixed. Pour into a large mixing bowl, add the chocolate-butter mixture, and stir well. Add as much additional melted chocolate as necessary to reach the proper consistency—the mixture should be crumbly but hold together when pressed into a ball. Press evenly into a 9-inch pie plate. Bake for approximately 10 minutes; watch so that it doesn't burn. Remove to a wire rack and let cool completely.

3. To make the filling, combine the sugar, cornstarch, and salt in a small bowl. In a heavy saucepan, bring the lemon juice and water to a boil. Add the sugar-cornstarch mixture, whisking until smooth, and cook over very low heat, stirring frequently, for approximately 30 minutes, until thick. Quickly whisk in the egg yolks and cook for 2 minutes longer. Remove from the heat, whisk in the butter, and let cool completely.

4. Mound the cooled filling in the prepared pie shell, and top with softly whipped cream.

Rosanna Jolis's Fig Tart with Pink Peppercorn Glaze

Rosanna's tart arrived in its black tart pan so the crust would stay intact. She set it in a huge hoop-handled wicker flower-gathering basket.

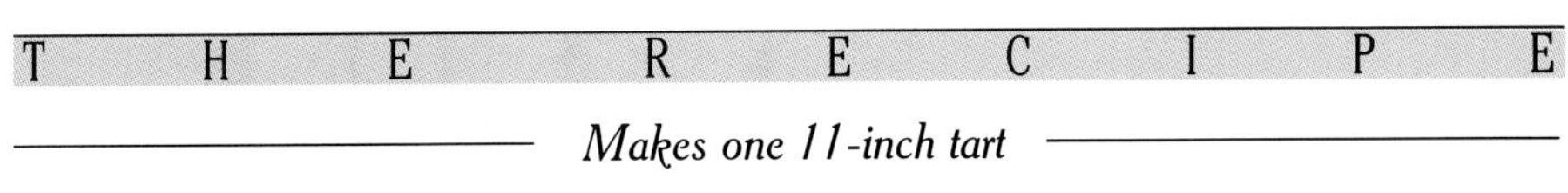

THE RECIPE

Makes one 11-inch tart

ONE 11-INCH PÂTE BRISÉE TART SHELL (PAGE 198), BAKED AND COOLED

Crème Pâtissière (Pastry Cream)

1 CUP MILK
¼ CUP GRANULATED SUGAR
3 TABLESPOONS ALL-PURPOSE FLOUR
¼ TEASPOON SALT
4 EGG YOLKS, LIGHTLY BEATEN
2 TEASPOONS VANILLA EXTRACT
2 TABLESPOONS UNSALTED BUTTER

Pink Peppercorn Glaze

1 CUP FIG PURÉE (ENGLISH FIG JAM)
2 TO 3 TABLESPOONS WATER
1 TABLESPOON CRUSHED PINK PEPPERCORNS

12 RIPE FRESH FIGS, QUARTERED

1. To make the crème pâtissière, heat the milk in a heavy saucepan until hot but not boiling. Combine the sugar, flour, and salt in a mixing bowl, and slowly add the hot milk. Pour this mixture back into the saucepan and bring to a boil over low heat, stirring constantly. Cook the mixture until smooth and very thick.

2. Off the heat, beat in the egg yolks, one at a time. Return the mixture to the heat and boil for about a minute, stirring vigorously. Remove from the heat and continue to beat until the mixture cools slightly. Stir in the vanilla and butter, blending thoroughly. Cover the pastry cream with plastic wrap directly touching its surface and let cool completely.

3. To make the glaze, put the fig purée in a saucepan over low heat and add just enough water to reach spreading consistency. Stir in the peppercorns and heat briefly.

4. To assemble the tart, stir 1 tablespoon of the glaze into the cooled pastry cream, for flavor, and spoon the cream evenly into the bottom of the tart shell. Arrange the quartered figs in concentric circles on top, and drizzle the remaining warm glaze over the figs. Refrigerate until ready to serve.

CHAPTER *11.*

Master Recipes & Techniques

OVEN
OVEN
OVEN

PÂTE BRISÉE (BASIC PIE CRUST)

I have been making pastry crusts since I was a little girl, and I think I have finally perfected the right proportion of butter to flour to water; my crust is almost always light, flaky, and tender, yet sturdy enough for pies, tarts, and tartlets. Using cold ingredients, chilling the pastry before rolling it out, rolling it out quickly and thinly, and baking at a high temperature are my other secrets.

The shortening I use most frequently is unsalted butter, but margarine, vegetable shortening, and lard can be used successfully with, of course, differences in taste, texture, and color (see the recipe for non-butter crust on page 203). I use all-purpose or unbleached flour and do not sift it for pastry. I keep flour stored in a large jar and measure it right from the jar using level cup or part-cup measures.

This crust, if worked correctly, does not "puff up." Tiny tartlets are shapely and freestanding, larger tart shells strong-sided. The crust browns very nicely in a 400° oven, and when brushed with a glaze turns glossy, yet never becomes tough. For custard-type pies, I often partially bake the pastry for ten to twelve minutes before adding the filling, to ensure a crisp bottom.

Makes two 8- to 10-inch tarts or single-crust pies, one 8- to 10-inch double-crust pie, or twelve 2½- to 3-inch tartlets

- 2½ CUPS ALL-PURPOSE FLOUR
- 1 TEASPOON SALT
- 1 TEASPOON GRANULATED SUGAR (OPTIONAL)
- 1 CUP (2 STICKS) COLD UNSALTED BUTTER, CUT INTO SMALL PIECES
- ¼ TO ½ CUP ICE WATER

---

1. Put the flour, salt, and sugar in the bowl of a food processor. All ingredients should be cold. Add the pieces of butter and process for approximately 10 seconds, or just until the mixture resembles coarse meal. (To mix by hand, combine the dry ingredients in a large mixing bowl. Using a pastry blender or two table knives, cut in the butter until the mixture resembles coarse meal.)

2. Add ice water, drop by drop, through the feed tube with the machine running, just until the dough holds together without being wet or sticky; do not process more than 30 seconds. Test the dough at this point by squeezing a small amount together. If it is crumbly, add a bit more water.

3. Turn the dough out onto a large piece of plastic wrap. Grasping the ends of the plastic wrap with your hands, as shown, press the dough into a flat circle with your fists. This makes rolling easier than if the pastry is chilled as a ball. Wrap the dough in the plastic and chill for at least an hour.

4. Lightly butter or spray with vegetable cooking spray the pie plate(s) or tart pan(s) you will be using. On a lightly floured board, roll out the pastry to a thickness of ⅛ inch. Place the pastry in the tart pan, pie plate, or pastry ring, which has been set on a parchment-lined baking sheet, and press it into the bottom edges and along the sides. Trim the pastry using scissors or a sharp paring knife, or by rolling a rolling pin across the top of the pan. (I often cut the pastry an inch or so higher than the edge of the tart pan and tuck this overhang to the inside of the pan for extra height and reinforcement.) Crimp or decorate the edges of the pastry, if desired, by any of the methods pictured on page 204. Chill the pastry-lined pan until ready to use. Unbaked pastry shells can be refrigerated, well wrapped in plastic, for up to 1 day; for longer storage, they can be frozen.

PREBAKED PASTRY SHELLS: To partially or completely bake unfilled pastry, preheat the oven to 375° to 400°. Carefully line the pastry with aluminum foil, pressing it into the corners and edges, and weight with beans, rice, or aluminum or ceramic weights, as illustrated on pages 200–201. Bake for 15 to 18 minutes (10 to 12 minutes for a partially baked shell). When the pastry begins to color around the edges, remove the foil and weights and continue to bake just until the pastry dries out and turns a light golden color for a partially baked shell, and a deeper amber for a fully baked shell. Let cool completely on a wire rack before filling. Baked shells can be stored in tightly covered plastic containers, or well wrapped, in the freezer.

MAKING PÂTE BRISÉE

*a.
Chilled ingredients are placed in the bowl of a food processor.*

*b.
Process until the mixture resembles coarse meal.*

*c.
Add ice water, drop by drop, with the machine running.*

*d.
Test the pastry; it should just hold together.*

*e.
Turn the dough out onto a sheet of plastic wrap.*

FORMING ROUND PÂTE BRISÉE TART SHELLS

Roll out the pastry to a thickness of 1/8-inch, fold it in half, place it in the tart ring, and carefully unfold. Trim the pastry to within 1 inch of the edge of the pan and tuck in the excess pastry to reinforce the edge.

Place the tart shell on a parchment-lined baking sheet. Mark the edges of the pastry with the back of a knife in a barber-pole design, if desired. Prick the bottom of the shell with the tines of a fork and chill before lining and weighting.

Line the shell with aluminum foil, pressing well into the bottom corners, and weight with beans, rice, or aluminum or ceramic weights. Carefully remove the weights when the pastry just begins to color around the edges. Continue baking until partially or fully baked, as desired.

After baking, remove the shell from the tart ring and let it cool completely on a rack. To facilitate handling, an extra tart pan bottom is used beneath each tart shell. Other types of pans or rings can be used: quiche pans with removable bottoms, petal- or heart-shaped tart rings, or even pie tins.

FORMING HEART-SHAPED PÂTE BRISÉE TART SHELLS

Roll out the pastry to a thickness of ⅛-inch. Using a heart-shaped tart ring, fit the pastry into the pan. Trim off the excess using a scissors, leaving 1 inch to tuck back inside as reinforcement. Crimp the edges, prick the bottom with the tines of a fork, and chill.

Carefully line the pastry with foil, weight with beans, rice, or aluminum or ceramic weights, and bake on a parchment-lined baking sheet.

FORMING PÂTE BRISÉE TARTLET SHELLS

Place tartlet pans on top of the pastry and, using a sharp knife, cut the pastry slightly larger than each pan. Press the pastry into the pans and, using the thumbs, cut off the excess. Place another tartlet pan of exactly the same size on top and press firmly.

The second pan will bake right on top and keep the pastry from puffing up. (This is an alternative to lining the shells with foil and weighting.) As soon as the tartlet shells come out of the oven, remove the top pan and let the shells cool on a rack.

PÂTE SUCRÉE
(BASIC SWEET CRUST)

Adding some sugar and two egg yolks alters the basic pâte brisée to create a sweet, slightly crunchy, but still tender crust that can be used in place of pâte brisée for fruit tarts and small dessert tartlets. Sweet crusts are generally not used for double-crust pies, only for tart and tartlet shells. Because the sugar and egg yolks soften the pastry, it is harder to roll out perfectly than the basic pâte brisée; however, patching is easy, because any tears can simply be pressed together. Longer chilling and careful handling should enable you to work this pastry successfully.

Makes two 8- to 10-inch tarts or single-crust pies, or twelve 2½- to 3-inch tartlets

- 2½ CUPS ALL-PURPOSE FLOUR
- 3 TABLESPOONS GRANULATED SUGAR
- 1 CUP (2 STICKS) COLD UNSALTED BUTTER, CUT INTO SMALL PIECES
- 4 TABLESPOONS ICE WATER
- 2 EGG YOLKS, LIGHTLY BEATEN

Follow the instructions for making pâte brisée (page 198), but slowly add the egg yolks at the same time as the ice water. Roll out and bake as directed.

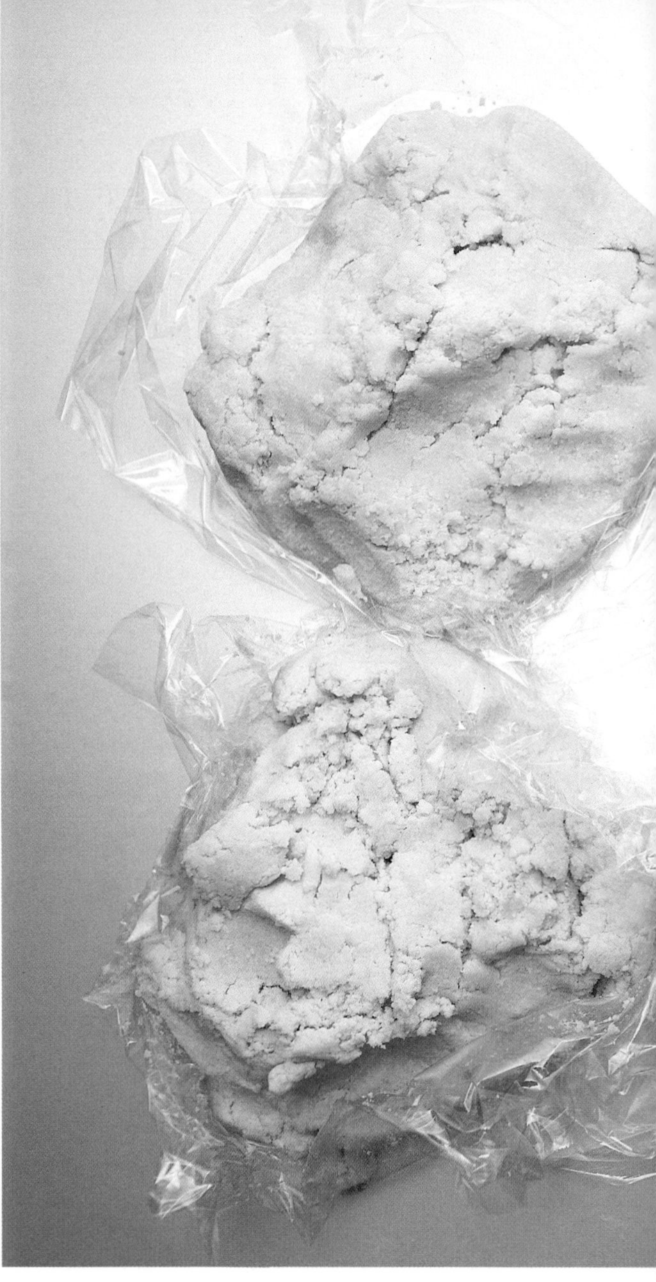

PÂTE SUCRÉE EXTRA
(SWEETER CRUST)

A bit more sugar and an additional egg yolk make this pastry more the consistency of a rich sugar cookie dough than the basic pâte sucrée. It is harder to roll out without tears and cracks, but it, too, can be patched and pressed together easily. It is especially good for making fruit tarts and tartlets with a rich, melt-in-your-mouth quality.

After you make the dough, let it rest in the refrigerator for about 15 to 20 minutes, but don't let it chill too long or it will be difficult to roll out. Roll the dough out on a generously floured board, using a floured rolling pin, so it does not stick. Like pâte sucrée, this pastry is used mainly for tarts and tartlets.

Makes two 8- to 10-inch tarts or single-crust pies, or twelve 2½- to 3-inch tartlets

- 2½ CUPS ALL-PURPOSE FLOUR
- ⅓ CUP GRANULATED SUGAR
- 1 CUP (2 STICKS) COLD UNSALTED BUTTER, CUT INTO SMALL PIECES
- 4 TABLESPOONS ICE WATER
- 3 EGG YOLKS, LIGHTLY BEATEN

Follow the instructions for making pâte brisée (page 198), slowly adding the egg yolks at the same time as the ice water. Roll out and bake as directed.

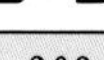

NON-BUTTER CRUST

This pastry is similar to pâte brisée in the proportion of flour to fat, and is perfect for those who prefer margarine, solid vegetable shortening, or lard (animal fat) to butter. I generally use all-butter pastry for my pies and tarts, but I do like a part butter–part margarine crust for lemon pie, a pure lard crust for old-fashioned apple or mincemeat pie, and a Crisco crust for blueberry or blackberry pie.

Some people claim that non-butter crusts are flakier and lighter than butter crusts, but I prefer the flavor of butter crusts for all-round use in making tarts, tartlets, and most pies. Of primary importance when making non-butter crusts is that all the ingredients be very cold. If during the mixing process they become at all sticky or soft, chill the whole bowl until everything is cold again. Pastry will not be flaky or tender or light if it is overworked or worked while the ingredients are too warm.

Makes two 8- to 10-inch single-crust pies or tarts, one 8- to 10-inch double-crust pie, or twelve 2½- to 3-inch tartlets

2½ CUPS ALL-PURPOSE FLOUR
1 TEASPOON SALT
½ TEASPOON GRANULATED SUGAR
1 CUP COLD VEGETABLE SHORTENING, LARD, OR MARGARINE, CUT INTO SMALL PIECES
½ CUP ICE WATER

Follow the instructions for making pâte brisée (page 198), rolling out and baking as directed.

Four types of pastry dough (clockwise from top left): *pâte lard, pâte brisée, pâte sucrée extra, and pâte sucrée.*

FORMING CRUST EDGES

Crimped Edge: *Using the thumb and forefinger of one hand, push with the thumb of the other hand to create a decorative edge.*

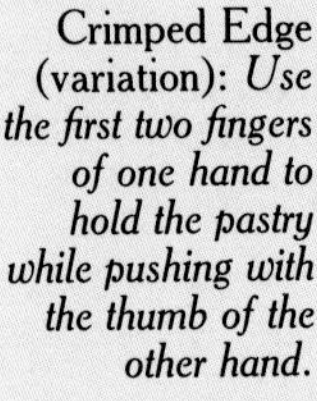

Crimped Edge (variation): *Use the first two fingers of one hand to hold the pastry while pushing with the thumb of the other hand.*

Crimped Edge with Fork Markings: *Use the thumb and forefinger of one hand to hold the pastry while pressing down and in with the tines of a fork.*

Leaf Edge: Cut *leaf shapes from pastry trimmings with the point of a sharp knife. Mark the leaves with veins using the back of the knife. Attach to the edge of the crust with a bit of cold water.*

Braided Edge: *Cut strips of pastry ¼-inch wide. Braid together and apply to the edge of the crust with a bit of cold water.*

NUT CRUST

This has become one of my favorite crusts because it's so easy and delicious. There is no rolling out involved and no need to line the shell with foil and weights. The crust, which resembles a cookie dough, is pressed right into the tart pan, chilled, and then baked.

I like to keep one or two baked nut crusts in the freezer for a very quickly assembled dessert. Once thawed, the shell can be filled with fresh berries and glazed, or mounded with a cream filling or mousse.

Makes two 8- to 10-inch tart shells or twelve 2½- to 3-inch tartlets

10 OUNCES FINELY CHOPPED ALMONDS, WALNUTS, PECANS, FILBERTS, OR MACADAMIA NUTS
1 CUP (2 STICKS) UNSALTED BUTTER, AT ROOM TEMPERATURE
⅓ CUP GRANULATED SUGAR
3 CUPS ALL-PURPOSE FLOUR
1 EGG, LIGHTLY BEATEN
1 TEASPOON ALMOND OR VANILLA EXTRACT

1. Preheat the oven to 350°. Butter the tart or tartlet pans you will be using.
2. Put all the ingredients in a large mixing bowl and mix until well blended, using an electric mixer or wooden spoon. Divide the mixture and press into the prepared pans. Chill for at least 30 minutes.
3. Bake the crust for 20 to 25 minutes, or until the shells are golden brown. Let cool on racks before filling.

Some of the basic ingredients for a nut crust—flour, ground nuts, sugar, and eggs. The dough is pressed into a quiche pan with a removable bottom and baked until it is a rich golden brown.

PUFF PASTRY
(PÂTE FEUILLETÉE)

For the most elegant tarts, galettes, and barquettes, this pastry, made with all cream, has no equal. During a baking class I taught at the Broadmoor Cooking School in Colorado Springs, at an altitude of seven thousand feet, my puff pastry rose to an airy height of 2¼ inches. Papillons made from the scraps were as light as any I have ever tasted, and long rectangular tart cases had such high sides that each tart required twice as much pastry cream as usual.

It is a pleasure to have such success, but making puff pastry does take a certain amount of skill and practice. Even now I sometimes have difficulty, because there are so many variables involved. What matters most is that the ingredients be measured accurately (I always weigh the flour), that no substitutions be made (no vegetable shortening for butter, half-and-half for cream), and that the pastry has time to rest and chill between rollings. For a less rich pastry, all water can be used, or half water and half heavy cream. Half-and-half does not seem to work as well as half cream and half water. I use either unbleached flour or a general all-purpose flour like Gold Medal. Heavy or bread flours should be avoided. Some bakers use part cake flour, but I get very satisfactory results with regular flour.

During the rest periods while the pastry is chilling, it is best to keep the pastry wrapped in plastic wrap, which helps maintain the essential moisture content of the dough. Correct baking is also very important; underbaking at too-low temperatures often accounts for tough, underpuffed results.

Makes approximately 2 pounds

- 1 POUND ALL-PURPOSE OR UNBLEACHED FLOUR, VERY ACCURATELY WEIGHED
- 1 POUND (4 STICKS) COLD UNSALTED BUTTER, CUT INTO SMALL PIECES
- 1 TEASPOON SALT
- 1 CUP HEAVY CREAM (OR ½ CUP HEAVY CREAM MIXED WITH ½ CUP ICE WATER)

1. In the bowl of a food processor or using the flat paddle of an electric mixer, mix ½ cup flour with the butter until very smooth. Shape the mixture into a flat square 1 inch thick, wrap well in plastic, and chill for at least 30 minutes.

2. Combine the salt with the remaining flour in a large mixing bowl and add the cream (or cream and water). Mix the dough well by hand or with an electric mixer; the dough will not be completely smooth but it should not be sticky. Shape it into a flat square 1½ inches thick, wrap in plastic, and chill, at least 30 minutes.

3. Remove the flour dough from the refrigerator. On a lightly floured board, roll the dough into a rectangle twice as long as the butter dough. Place the butter dough in the center, fold up the ends to completely encase the butter dough, and seal the edges by pinching them together. Wrap well in plastic and chill for at least 30 minutes, so that the dough achieves the same temperature throughout.

4. Remove the dough from the refrigerator and, on a lightly floured board, roll it out into a large rectangle approximately ½ inch thick. Fold the dough into thirds, aligning the edges carefully and brushing off any excess flour. The object is to ensure that the butter is distributed evenly throughout so that the pastry will puff evenly when baked. Wrap the dough and chill it for at least 30 minutes. This completes one turn.

5. Repeat this process five more times; classic puff pastry gets six turns, creating hundreds of layers of butter between layers of the flour dough (729 to be exact). Use as little flour as possible when rolling out the dough, and always brush off any excess. (I use a 4-inch brush for this.) Remember to let the dough rest for at least 30 minutes in the refrigerator between turns, or 15 minutes in the freezer. This chilling makes the rolling out much easier and it keeps the layers of butter of equal thickness.

6. By the sixth and final turn, the dough should be very smooth, with no lumps of butter visible. Wrap the pastry in plastic wrap and refrigerate until ready to use (up to 2 days), or freeze for future use. I usually divide the dough into 1-pound pieces and freeze it that way.

(continued on page 208)

MAKING PUFF PASTRY

a.
A butter dough is mixed. Next, a flour-and-cream dough is mixed. Both are refrigerated until well chilled.

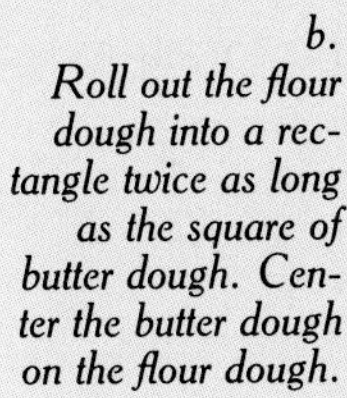

b.
Roll out the flour dough into a rectangle twice as long as the square of butter dough. Center the butter dough on the flour dough.

c.
Fold the edges of the flour dough up over the butter dough to encase it.

d.
Roll out the combined dough into a rectangle.

e.
Fold the rectangle into thirds, and brush away any excess flour. This completes one turn.

FORMING PUFF PASTRY TART SHELLS

Use a ruler to measure out a rectangle and to even off the sides and ends. Cut ½-inch-wide strips and use cold water to apply them to the edge of the rectangle, overlapping the ends as shown to form a raised edge.

Cut out two hearts of equal size. Using a slightly smaller heart shape as a guide, cut an even edge ½-inch wide from one of the hearts. Using cold water, apply this to the edge of the other heart as illustrated to form an even rim.

Prick only the bottom with the tines of a fork. Very carefully glaze only the edges with an egg yolk and cream mixture. Shown here are the finished cases, ready for baking.

(continued from page 206)

RECTANGULAR TART SHELLS: To make rectangular tart shells from puff pastry, roll out the pastry into a rectangle at least 20 inches long and approximately ⅛ inch thick. Using a ruler as your guide, cut the edges with a sharp knife so that the pastry measures the desired size (I generally make these 4 × 18 inches). From the remaining pastry, cut three strips ½ inch wide and as long as the tart.

Place the rectangle on a parchment-lined or water-sprayed baking sheet. Build up the edges by pasting two strips on the long edges with water. Cut the third strip into two strips that will fit the shorter edges and attach with a bit of cold water, overlapping the ends. Prick the entire inside bottom of the pastry shell with the tines of a fork (this prevents uneven puffing). Carefully line *only* the bottom with aluminum foil, and weight with beans, rice, or aluminum or ceramic weights. (Be careful not to weight the edges.) Refrigerate, covered, for at least 30 minutes.

Preheat the oven to 400°. Remove the pastry from the refrigerator and brush the uncovered edges with a glaze of 1 egg yolk mixed with 2 teaspoons cream or water. Bake for 12 to 15 minutes, or until the edges have puffed and begun to brown. Remove the weights and foil, and continue to bake until the entire shell is light golden brown. Let cool completely on a wire rack.

HEART-SHAPED TART SHELLS: To make heart-shaped tart shells from puff pastry, roll out the dough to a thickness of approximately ⅛ inch. Using a very sharp paring knife and a heart-shaped pan, flan ring, or cardboard cutout of the desired size, cut out two hearts. Place one on a parchment-lined or water-sprayed baking sheet, and cut an even ½-inch rim from the edge of the remaining heart. Place this rim carefully and exactly on top of the other, pasting it on with water. Prick the inside bottom with the tines of a fork, carefully line only the bottom with aluminum foil, and weight with beans, rice, or aluminum or ceramic weights. Refrigerate, glaze, and bake as described above.

QUICK PUFF PASTRY

This is a fast and simple alternative to classic puff pastry. I recommend it for galettes and free-form fruit tarts. The butter is cut very roughly into the flour, and turns are accomplished much more rapidly. It is still important to work quickly with cold ingredients and to chill the dough, letting it rest between turns. The dough does not rise as much as the classic version, but the flavor is excellent. It is not as rich as puff pastry made from cream.

Makes approximately 2 pounds

3¾ CUPS ALL-PURPOSE OR UNBLEACHED FLOUR
1 TEASPOON SALT
1 POUND (4 STICKS) COLD UNSALTED BUTTER
1 TO 1¼ CUPS ICE WATER

1. Mix the flour and salt in a large chilled stainless steel bowl. Cut the butter into very thin pieces. Using a pastry blender, or working with your fingertips, cut the butter into the flour until the butter is in very small lumps, about ½ inch in diameter. (A food processor will not work for this pastry, because it tends to cut the butter into too-fine pieces.)

2. Stir in the water, a little at a time, pressing the dough together. Turn the dough out onto a well-floured board and roll it into a rough rectangle. The dough will be very crumbly. Fold it into thirds, and give the dough a quarter turn to the right. Roll into a large rectangle and fold into thirds again. This completes the first double turn. Remove any excess flour with a wide brush. Wrap the dough in plastic and chill for 30 minutes.

3. Repeat this rolling and turning process two more times, chilling well between turns. With each turn the dough will become smoother and easier to handle. This puff pastry, like pâte feuilletée, requires six full turns (accomplished as three double turns) before it is complete.

4. Roll out and bake as directed for classic puff pastry, following the directions on page 208. Store the dough wrapped well in plastic in the refrigerator for up to 2 days, or freeze for future use.

Cut the butter into the flour until only small chunks remain.

Turn the mixture out onto a floured board and roll it out into a rough rectangle. The dough will be quite crumbly.

Fold the rectangle into thirds as shown, give it a quarter-turn to the right, and roll it out again.

Fold the dough again into thirds, to complete one double turn. Remove excess flour with a wide brush.

G L A Z E S

Glazes can be lovely, shining finales for the tops of fruit and berry tarts and tartlets. For years I had been satisfied with apricot and red currant glazes, but recently I discovered that other jellies can be used equally well. While working on this book, I experimented with sour cherry jelly made from the Montmorency cherries we grow in great abundance. To my delight, the jelly was a beautiful pale pink, with a unique flavor. I also used our quinces, which we had most often used for preserves and chutneys, to make quince jelly of several different hues—the riper quinces produced a deep pink jelly and the less ripe fruits a more golden, paler jelly. The quince jelly had an extremely high pectin content, and we found that quince syrup, cooked just to a point before it reached the jelly stage, was an excellent thickening and sweetening agent for whipped cream fillings. Crab apple jelly also had lovely qualities—high pectin content, a glorious deep amber color, and an interesting flavor—that made it a perfect glaze.

We also made jellies from the berries that we were using to fill a tart or from other fruits that matched them in color. For example, the blackberry tart needed a very dark glaze. I had black currant syrup in my freezer, and turned it into a glistening glaze that was just the right color and complemented the flavor of the blackberries. Orange tarts were brushed with a glaze made from the juice of highly flavored temple oranges. Lemon juice, too, was boiled with sugar to make a lemon-flavored glaze for several of the lemon tarts.

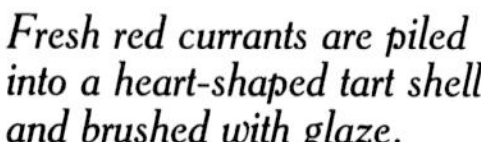

Fresh red currants are piled into a heart-shaped tart shell and brushed with glaze.

BASIC GLAZE RECIPE

Makes 1 cup

1 CUP JELLY OR JAM

2 TABLESPOONS COINTREAU, GRAND MARNIER, OR COGNAC (OPTIONAL)

Heat the jelly until melted. If using jam, heat until melted and press through a fine sieve. Then simmer gently for 3 to 5 minutes—do not boil. Remove from the heat and stir in the liqueur, if desired. Let cool slightly, then brush or spoon over fruit.

BASIC JELLY RECIPE

Makes approximately 2 to 2½ pints

4 CUPS WHOLE BERRIES OR STEMMED AND SEEDED FRUIT, CUT UP

GRANULATED SUGAR

1. Mash the berries and cook with a small amount of water (about ½ cup) until very soft. When cooking fruit, use enough water to just cover and cook until very soft. Pour into a jelly bag (I use flannel bags from England, but a fine linen dishcloth or a pillowcase will work). Let the juice drip from the berries or fruit, without squeezing or pressing. This gives the clearest jelly.

2. To each cup of juice, add 1 cup sugar. Bring to a boil and, keeping the temperature constant at a full rolling boil, skim off any scum. Cook until the jelly coats a metal spoon or until a small amount "sheets" on a saucer. Store in covered sterilized jars in the refrigerator.

BASIC SYRUP RECIPE

Proceed as for jelly but cook the juice only until the liquid begins to thicken. The mixture should remain liquid and should not jell. Store in covered containers in the freezer.

Fruit glazes (clockwise from top right): *quince, apricot, crab apple, sour cherry, grenadine, orange, red currant, and black currant* (center).

INDEX

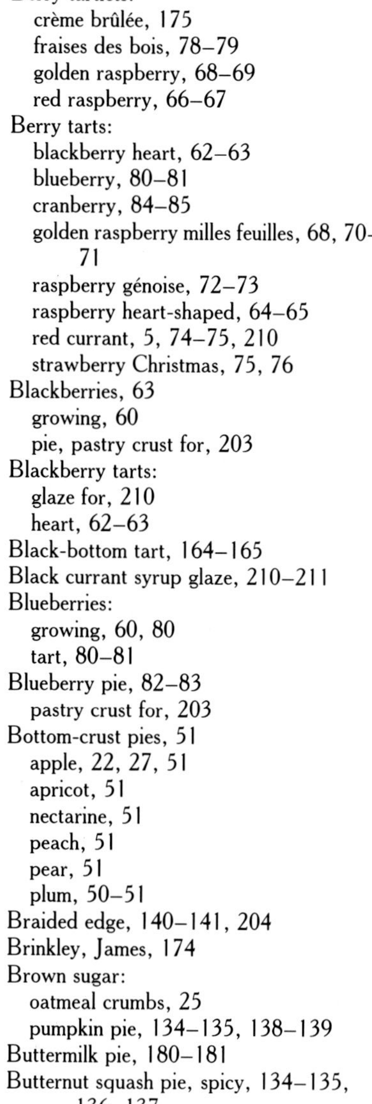

D

E

F

W